What agents are saying

In this no-holds-barred compilation, Pam and Rich tell you how it is on the front lines of a high-level professional real estate agent's practice. Their fantastic storytelling ability lends itself to this fresh look at how agents can conduct their businesses. My hat is off to Pam and Rich for showing us that the real estate industry of the future will be dominated by agents who have evolved past simple salesmanship and adopted an ownership mentality toward their business, their clients, and most importantly, the ethics that guide their decisions.

—*Craig Owen, Team Leader, Keller Williams Realty*

A fun, sensible approach to focusing your real estate career for success—right from the start. I highly recommend that every agent who is ready for their career to take off read this book!

—*Wendi Harrelson, Team Leader, Keller Williams Realty*

Excellent! Pam and Rich offer invaluable information to both seasoned professionals as well as those just entering the real estate profession... a true gem.

—*Tom Vincent, RE/MAX North*

Anyone thinking of being successful in real estate should give themselves a jump start and read *Scorpion in the Bathtub*.

—*Patti Bailey (Agent for 25 years), Keller Williams Realty*

Real stories for real people. Every established agent has had one of these situations happen to them. Knowing how to ask the right questions will certainly help us all be more successful.

—*Renee Rogers, Keller Williams Realty*

You have mastered the art of educating the agent who wants to earn more than NAR's "average." I would offer this advice to anyone considering this business: In this challenging business of real estate, you must start with a strong foundation and continue to build on it with quality education gleaned from successful sources or you are doomed to failure. Pam and Rich have taken a successful career and distilled it into a well-organized and entertaining book and laid it at your feet. Do the "right thing" and make this great real estate tool a well-used resource in your business library. Learn from it and you will earn well beyond the income of the "average" agent.

—*Thom Perdue, RE/MAX Preferred*

You could not have hit the nail on the head any better.... This will be a great tool for both new and seasoned agents. I hope that as people read this book they will realize what they can do to grow their business and that they choose to do something about it.... P.S. I started to read while at a complete standstill on the highway and found myself so involved in it that the man in the 4x4 truck had to honk at me to get me to realize that everyone but me was ready to move. That's when I realized...this needs to be on a CD!

—*Angela Diaz, Keller Williams Realty*

This is one of the most useful and enjoyable books for real estate agents that I've ever read. Pam and Rich set out to be successful in the business of real estate. Along the way, they made a few mistakes, and learned from them, as well as from other successful agents. In *Scorpion*, they share their experiences and reveal ways to build a productive and satisfying career in real estate. Get two copies, since one of them is going to get dog-eared and marked up and the other will make a great gift for your favorite real estate agent.

—*Robin Rogers, Legacy Group*

Practical advice from experienced agents who have learned to look past the transaction. Real estate is a business built on relationships and an enormous amount of communication. The easy storytelling format included with references to real life experiences and specific books for recommended reading, make this a must read for the real estate warrior. I couldn't put it down.

— *Laurie Charles, ERA Legend Real Estate*

Scorpion in the Bathtub

Profits and Perils of Real Estate

Pam and Rich O'Bryant

Scorpion in the Bathtub

Profits and Perils of Real Estate

The opinions expressed in this manuscript are solely the opinions of the author and do not represent the opinions or thoughts of the publisher. The author represents and warrants that s/he either owns or has the legal right to publish all material in this book.

All Rights Reserved
Copyright © 2006 Pam & Rich O'Bryant

This book may not be reproduced, transmitted, or stored in whole or in part by any means, including graphic, electronic, or mechanical without the express written consent of the publisher except in the case of brief quotations embodied in critical articles and reviews.

Outskirts Press
http://www.outskirtspress.com

ISBN-10: 1-59800-891-9
ISBN-13: 978-1-59800-891-3

Outskirts Press and the "OP" logo are trademarks belonging to Outskirts Press, Inc.

Printed in the United States of America

Contents

Your Career: What's It Worth to You?	i
Foreword: The Business Owner Mindset	iii
Acknowledgements	viii
The Best Stories Aren't Just True, They're Typical	viii
I Buyers	**11**
1 Buyers Aren't Liars	14
We Found "It," Pam!	21
Finding a Home for a Bear	24
You Have To Ask	29
2 Great Models Beat Great Brains	33
Who Else is in the Back Seat?	38
Having to Rent is a State of Mind	42
Two for the Price of One	45
3 Picking Keepers	48
Is My Buyer First in Line?	53
You Can get Bit from the Strangest Places	57
Dispossessed and Repossessed	62
II Listings, Mixed Blessings of the Real Estate Gods	**65**
4 It isn't Sold Until It's Sold	68
5 Know When to Fold	77
Icons and Armchairs	78
6 Not Every Deal will Work	83
Termites	84
Finnegan's Saga	85
Leave Before You List It	91
Fear of Being in Charge	93
7 How to Build a Winning Team	96
A Hot Day and a Cool Deal	98
The Golden Rule of Reciprocity	100
Watch Your Step	103

III The Closing Celebration — 107
8 Moving to the Next Phase — 108
Do It Right, You Make More Money — 111
9 The Truth is a Matter of Perspective — 117
God Will Provide — 118
"Are You Married?" — 120
10 Strong Files make Smooth Deals — 125
Inspections Are a Pain — 129
Some People Aren't Ready to Own a Home — 134
11 Keep Your Head and Commission — 138
Money does not Equal Taste—or Good Sense! — 141
Scorpion in the Bathtub — 145

IV The Lead Machine — 149
12 There Are Only Six Ways to Make Money — 150
13 How to Build a Farm — 153
Sex and Tax Valuations — 158
A Client's Need is a Marketer's Gold — 159
14 Circle of Influence as a Major Profit Center — 161
26 Miles and $9K — 163
Wedding Day — 165

V Work Toward Mailbox Money — 169
15 Build It Right and It Will Last — 170
16 Rentals are a Lot of Work — 174
Always Check the Back Door — 179
17 Planning for Success From the Start — 181
Concluding Thoughts — 184
Appendix — 185

Your Career: What's It Worth to You?

Or, Why You Can't Afford Not to Put into Practice the Lessons and Stories Found in This Book

The real estate industry is changing daily. If you read trade magazines and the newspaper you will see career options, marketing strategies, and technological options change as fast as the view from an airport escalator.

What you and I are facing is a two-fold problem. First, which strategies do we as individuals want to implement to make money in this shifting industry? Second, how can we get the information we need to do this in a format that makes sense to us? The second part is just as important as the first and the reason you need this book.

No matter how good the information, if the reader just can't wade through a book it will not help. This book begins with a story and has stories in every section to demonstrate each point. Storytelling has for eons been the preferred method for passing on information. The stories have another function: they are fun.

The point is that a book has to be fun from page one or it will not help you. This one is, and it will.

Foreword: The Business Owner Mindset

This book is about being successful, but the first question everyone asks is why so many fail? I have some very strong feelings about that question. Most agents don't know enough about marketing, operations, and finance as these apply to a real estate practice, but *that* doesn't cause them to fail. These can be taught, and I will begin your education in a few pages. Real, can't-get-around-it, failure starts with a person not dedicated to "getting it right." And that is not a thing that can be bought or a course I can teach. It is the first component of the key mindset.

I call this the Business Owner Mindset (BOM) and I can't think of a way for any person to be successful without it. Here is what I mean: I had to see myself as a businessperson *before* I could become one. Life works this way. Thoughts that lead to plans come before plans that develop into systems. It is finally the systems that generate continuing streams of profit. Henry Ford is often quoted as having said, "If you think you can do a thing or think you can't do a thing, you're right." What I envision for myself, my business, and my life I can bring into reality. On the other hand, it is impossible for me to bring anything into being until I can envision it, plan it, and schedule the steps to get it done.

The BOM expresses itself on three major levels and each is necessary; each adds something irreplaceable.

The most visible level of this mindset is the attention to detail. The nuts and bolts of the business have to be taken care of. Every buyer, every seller, every client conversation has to be handled according to the system and with the correct dialog. Here, chance and innovation are considered enemies. Scripts are things to be practiced until they become normal conversation. They never sound like something I am trying out or have somewhat memorized. They have become the way I talk in the target situation. Marketing is planned and systemized to the point that it happens on time and in the same professional manner every time. If a marketing piece is scheduled to be sent the first week of the month, it is sent out on the first Thursday and arrives on the first Saturday. Clients can count on it.

Actually, not all great business people are as organized as they have to be; still, they make organization happen. Many outsource the repetitive tasks or *hire* people who are organized. Remember *getting it right* is the goal, not *being right*.

The second level of the BOM is the ability, and the inner feeling of necessity, to look at the business as it will look at the end of years one, three, five,…and retirement. The owner knows that it is her vision that will create the business plan and her plan that will allow the business to develop. The owner knows it is her standards of honesty, quality, and care for others that will inform the entire entity she is creating. The expression of this focus governs the experience of all those whom she serves, employs, and is a role model for.

Finally, the business owner has a vision of what the business will do for the owner. A true owner is a balanced person and understands that the business funds his life and enhances his life experiences, but is not his life. This mindset is one of perspective, and the owner knows what he wants from the business. He grasps the fact that his life will progress on a directed course even after he stops doing real estate sales. He believes in his heart that he is in control and has choices.

Living up to these three levels of business ownership every day seems to be a challenge, but the emphasis is on *seems*. In reality, I can tell the days I live up to it from those that I don't. Hey, no one is perfect. The days I get it done are creative busy ones. My precious clients get the service they deserve and leads come in for new business. Time flies while I have fun. On the *other* days, those when I miss the BOM standard, I just get through, I'm not as attentive, and I'm glad when they are over. Someone not excited about her business and habitually just getting through her days is a mediocre performer. You should be careful to avoid all her habits, traits, and outlooks.

Of course, everyone can teach us something.

In this book I begin talking about buyers, sellers, and selling real estate. This is the stuff of a real estate practice. If you change the terminology to generating leads and providing a service or product, then we are talking about every business on the planet from GM to the shoeshine boy. An agent is not an agent until she generates a lead to work with; a dentist is not a dentist until she generates a lead to sit in the big chair. This is how it works. Our ideal business owner knows she has two jobs every day. The first is lead generation and the second is the service she provides to clients. In the following pages I will relate these two functions to buyers, sellers, and selling real estate.

You may be wondering (I hope you are anyway) about how to start developing this mystical Business Owner Mindset in the real world. May I make a few suggestions, dear colleague? Start by making your business visible.

Go to your bank and open a checking account for your business. You don't need to call it a business account; if you do the bank will probably charge more. Never waste money on something meaningless. Then get a new credit card that you will only use for your business expenses. Of course you probably have enough cards already, so just clear off one of those. Once it's at zero, use it only for business expenses.

Doing these things right at the start is showing *yourself* you have a business. Of course it is practical to have your expenses segregated for tax purposes. But that is secondary. We actually got American Express Platinum *Business* Cards; I wanted everyone (including myself) to see something with business written on it when I pulled out my card.

The next thing you should do is spend an evening reading this book; it is short on purpose. Then get focused on which two strategies you will use to generate leads and start to put your business together along the lines of the model I discuss in the last chapter. I have put the organization part at the end because you will need to have an idea of how you want to practice real estate *before* you start to organize it. However, your business is not organized until the organizational chart is made, the scripts collected, the marketing developed and costed. Don't worry; I go into great detail on how all of this is set up later.

After the set-up, you are rolling, but you are not trained. In fact, now is the time I have to tell you a secret about business: I am still learning it! Ten years from now I will be in a different industry, maybe a different state, but I will still be learning business— and so will you. Every goal I reach instantly becomes a starting point for the next goal and every goal requires some new skill, or system, or knowledge set, and usually all three. You will never finish.

Because successful business people, people with The Business Owner Mindset, have to continue learning to complement their skill set and fulfill their vision of themselves and their business, I have listed a few books and resources in an appendix. This is not a list of the all-time best books in the world, but I think it is a start. Take a minute to read what I have to say about them and decide if any of them float your boat. You don't have to read them, but you will need to read some at least as good. Without study, you sentence yourself to making *all the mistakes* instead of learning from the mistakes of others.

Finally, I need to mention two housekeeping points about this book. When I use the word we, I'm usually talking about my husband, Rich, and me. We built our real estate practice together and enjoy each other's company—a lot. To this day we have a business conference on the deck with a glass of wine almost daily. The other issue is the necessity of using the pesky words he and she and their derivatives. Fabulous agents, lenders, and business people come in both sexes. As you have already seen, I have decided to use the pronouns interchangeably except where gender is specific such as in the stories that follow every chapter.

At the end of each chapter, and sometimes in the middle of one, I tell a story or two. These have several uses. Most obviously, they give examples of what I have discussed in the chapter and often points from other chapters as well. Because these are all actual events that happened to Rich and me, some of them don't fit neatly in to any particular compartment. Personally, I think a good story justifies itself. Another point for you to consider is the use of stories in your practice. You will learn from them, and clients can too.

We have found that clients relate to stories better than lectures and can use them to communicate to us. The other day a new agent called Rich with a client problem and he told her the story Finding a House for a Bear (see Chapter 1). She, in turn, told it to the troublesome client. It clicked, and the client called back the next day and said he knew what his "bear" was. More importantly, the agent got him under contract that very weekend.

Acknowledgements

Everyone owes a debt of thanks to innumerable numbers of people for helping them become the individuals they are, and Rich and I are no exceptions. My training in real estate began at the dinner table. When both parents are licensed real estate brokers guess what you hear all your life?

The biggest influence on this book has been our coach of nine years, Joe Stumpf. The knowledge, insight, and respect for clients that he has brought to our practice have been invaluable. I doubt we would have stayed in the business if Joe had not entered our lives. Our broker, Mark Willis, has been a constant source of inspiration and motivation. It is sustaining to know that a leader of this quality believes in you. While Joe has provided our outlook on client care, the brain trust for organization is Gary Keller, founder of Keller Williams Realty. The two years we spent in his seminars with a small group of dedicated, high-producing agents allowed us to see this industry as the awesome business opportunity that it is.

While these industry leaders have been key to our development, we must reserve our biggest thanks and humble acknowledgement to the hundreds of unique, interesting, and usually wonderful clients that made it happen. They taught us, fed us, and are building our future—thanks a million, guys; see you at the next client event!

The Best Stories Aren't Just True, They're Typical

Jane Doeson entered the real-estate office square-shouldered. Her well-fitting emerald-green dress, accented with a red designer silk scarf, exuded professional poise. She knew that her understated jewelry highlighted critical focal points on an impressive package—Jane Doeson.

Confidence radiated as she walked through the large, mostly empty, office to the packed computer room. She caught my eye in the hall just before the door, as she adjusted her convincing smile. Jane's first words tumbled out to the friendly clutch inside the narrow room.

"I got the job," came out and was followed by an almost sing-song, "I'm First American's new marketing rep for the northeast area!" The clutch gave friendly, if obligatory, oos and aahs.

Jane is a real sales talent. Before leaving, she, rather skillfully I thought, lined up a couple of transactions and several firm commitments. As a marketing rep, Jane was now on salary plus a small commission and able to pay her bills regularly. This had been a problem during the eight hard months she had invested in her real estate career. Her dream had died as her security needs had increased.

It reminded me of a honeybee. Not bees in general, but a particular one. One I felt responsible for.

Early in spring on the first warm Saturday, I inadvertently let a bee into the house. Having lived on a farm for a short time, I have a lot of respect for the job bees do and I felt bad about messing up this little lady's day. (All worker bees are female. You learn these things on a farm.)

I did everything short of swatting her and throwing her out the back door, which I left open. She could see the world through the wall of windows in our living room and wanted to get at it all, right now. No detours. Nothing I could do would change her infinite focus on the whole world and get her to see the open door close by, offering the predictable way to her objective.

Jane entered the real estate business like a force of nature. I watched her go to training classes religiously; I taught a lot of them. She did some farming to her neighborhood, mailed some calendars to her huge circle of friends and family, held a few open houses, called on some For Sale By Owners, and spent her savings before she made any real money. Now this talented person had given up on a career that literally has no income ceiling in return for a salary-plus box.

We had discussed focus. I had given her my mini-class in doing just two things at the mastery level to build a business, but she couldn't seem to narrow down. Everything looked interesting to her, and every training class gave her a new strategy. She must be a classic in a buffet line.

I began to be concerned for her when she caught me on a break in my contracts class and was visibly perturbed. She looked like she had been lied to.

"Open houses do not work," came out in an aggravated sputter. I asked her how many she had done.

"Three."

My comment that a lot of agents (me among them) make a lot of money with open houses did not seem to reach her. She knew she was smart and couldn't countenance the possibility that she did not know how to do them well enough. She had gone to a class on how to do them and they seemed very simple. If you are convinced, and she was, that an open house is just a few signs and sitting in a strange living room for three hours watching TV, then you're going to have a problem with open houses. Mastery of anything is a higher bar than most of us think.

This story was repeated. She did a mailing and nobody called. She called FSBOs and no one wanted her to come list their home. Nothing worked. Of course, Jane did the right stuff, just too much of it all and not enough of any one thing. A lot of activity and only a little planning makes an agent broke.

On Sunday, I swept up my determined bee from the floor in front of the picture window.

—Pam O'Bryant

1 Buyers

Emotions are in charge

Emotions control every buying decision. This is the great fact of all sales, and as an agent, you are in sales. I don't say this to be argumentative. The sooner you understand deep down that it is *heart and gut*, not head and logic, the better you will meet your clients' needs and make more money. Facts do play a role, but not the one you think. If you listen carefully to your clients, you will hear the reasons they are going to use to justify whatever emotional decision they later make.

The sequence you will hear over and over from buyers is the rock-hard logic of what they want or plan to do. Then you show them a few houses and they do whatever their emotional selves tell them to do. Afterward, usually on the way back to the office to write the offer, they begin digging out the logic again. They have to justify what they just committed to do. Remember, only a few scant minutes ago you watched them mentally buy the house and you knew that no logic was in the room at the time. They simply loved the place. You had made certain that it was one they could have (affordable payments, still on the market, etc.), and they fell for it. No one will ever admit to an emotional decision, but everyone does it.

Use their facts for your close

Facts can't be just pushed aside. Often they are very useful in a close. Almost every buyer has a list of what he or she has to have. Wait until you read the story about the guy with the bear. I'm convinced they do most of this because they think it is expected of them. Listen, always listen, and help them. Often, reciting the features they said they wanted helps a close and gets the paperwork done. However, this emotional burst of buying activity, which buyers try to hide with logic, is not the first buyer emotion we must handle. The first and most important emotion is seldom mentioned.

Fear is the predominant emotion in all real estate transactions. Every buyer and seller is in fear during the process. Who wouldn't be? They don't do real estate every day.

The unknown is not it. No one is afraid of the unknown. When I was a kid I picked up snakes and turtles and whatever. I did that because they were unknown and interesting. As an adult, I don't feel the urge to pick up many snakes any more. I know something about them now. For most adults, it is the same feeling about real estate. They know just enough to be a danger to themselves and at some level they believe it. You, the professional agent on the scene, must manage it for them. It is like going to the office of a great dentist.

Relaxing is not a term associated with dental work (or real estate) in the minds of the general public. You can take my word on this. But this does not mean the problem is insoluble.

The other day I went to my scheduled teeth cleaning at Dr. H's office. It was a subtle, choreographed production. The waiting room was empty. I knew I would be seen quickly. I had to be next; no one else was there. Once I was in "the chair," the assistant explained the process, showed me a short film that explained the process, and took an unconscionable number of x-rays. These people were not winging it. They had a process that was so firmly set in place they even had it on DVD. Surrounded by this convincing client-care system, I did just what it was designed to allow me to do. I relaxed.

Of course as I left the office I noticed four treatment rooms. I had not been "next"; Dr. H just managed the four of us patients well. The DVD was just a canned presentation from a dentist marketing operation. The point is the client-care system he put into place did the necessary fear management to make the client comfortable. More to the point, I will keep the next scheduled appointment and not shop around for a cheaper dentist. Dr. H is not cheap, and I don't care.

Managing fear is Job One

We will get into managing fear in huge detail in the coming chapters. For now think about listening to your clients. Managing fear starts here.

Imagine you are a young, single buyer. You drive up to the real estate office, and it is huge. Dozens of people are running around and all of them seem to have something important to do. You just want to buy a house. The agent you have an appointment with comes to the lobby and greets you in less than five minutes. He takes you to a quiet office, listens to all your questions and answers them. Next he asks some probing ones you hadn't thought of. You get a presentation from a 18-page booklet on the home-buying process that is personalized to his practice, and then he *gives it to you* for future reference. Can you see yourself relaxing? You are in a system, dealing with a professional, and can see that this home-buying thing may not be so bad after all. At least it's organized!

One great truism of sales is that if you want to impress a person with how smart you are, let him talk. Ask questions and shut up. After he answers, tie him down with the old "what I heard you say is…." You reword what they said and they think you are brilliant.

One final general statement about homebuyers: these guys are the foot soldiers of the market. What they like creates the latest trend. What they will pay controls price appreciation. Where they want to live determines the next hot neighborhood. Knowing how buyers will react is key information for your marketing, staging listings to sell, and business planning.

Next, let's explore how to handle buyers up close and personal, how to listen to and interpret their language, and what they really mean.

1 Buyers Aren't Liars

(But They Don't Tell the Truth Either)

What do you want? This sounds like such a simple question. But it isn't. It stumps everyone. The other day I was in McDonald's; I actually got out of my car and went in. Too many cars were stuck in the drive-through lane. In front of me stood a young guy and his girlfriend; their love was so obvious it was almost to the point of olfactory. I'm not complaining about this part, love is okay; but it took them three minutes to select lunch from the overhead menu. They had difficulties knowing what they wanted at Mickey Ds. Stupefying. Someday they will buy a house, select a career, decide to have kids, and figure out a retirement plan. Oh, boy.

The real estate menu issue

Every agent on the planet at some point has wondered why buyers can't just say what they want, would like to have, can afford, and where they want it. Think of the time it would save if real estate desires could be as simple as "hold the sauce, onions, and pickle, and super-size me." It can't be this easy, but you would think it could. Like a menu, there are a limited number of issues to deal with.

We want their needs and wants first. This sounds simple enough, but don't kid yourself. The idea that they really have two lists of things strikes most people as funny and requires explanation. They think House Perfect is out there and you will find it for them.

Reality check: even if they hire an architect and build it from the ground up, on a lot they selected, the house will not be perfect. Life does not work that way.

What you're trying to discover are the hard requirements that a house has to have. I use language like the following:

"Well, Jim, here is what I mean by features that it has to have. If a house were ten thousand dollars under market and did not have this feature, you would still not be interested in looking at it. A feature that you would like to have is one that you could live without if the deal was a good one."

After going through this sort of dialog a few times we generally start making headway. Before we move on to looking at homes and discussing the critical buying signs, we must look at our least-favorite upfront activity.

The dreaded dollar question

Do you enjoy asking a person you have just met, "How much do you make per month and how much debt do you have?" Of course not; we *hate* to ask those questions. Our mothers taught us better than that. On the other hand, every agent has shown a nice couple houses all weekend long only to find out on Monday that they couldn't rent a porta-potty without a co-signer. For me, the bottom line is that both of these situations are less than optimal. But I have a system to get the information while staying out of the line of fire.

Remember the dentist's office experience I mentioned at the beginning of this section? I experienced a *process*. Three different people visited with me, doing their different tasks while showing the DVD and taking x-rays. It was a system that managed my fear and got all the information Dr. H (that is really what they call him in the office) needed before he even saw me. It is easy to sound smart when you have the critical data ahead of time. Well that is what a system can do for you, and what you need in your real estate practice. Let me describe how this works in real estate. First I give them something to drink, then I get to work.

Buyer training sequence

After the initial meet-and-greet phase, I discuss my relationship with whoever referred them; most clients are referrals. This process is called Triangle for Trust. Doing it well will make you a lot of money. It works on a simple principle: they know and trust the person who referred them to me. That person knows and trusts me; therefore, they can feel comfortable trusting me. I want to establish this situation of mutual trust right at the beginning. It is the first step toward managing their fear. It also sets up the referral model I want to establish in their minds. A well-trained client normally has a lifetime value of four referrals up to "unlimited" if you can maintain mind share (much more on that later).

The next step is the buyer book. We wrote an 18-page booklet on the steps of the home-buying process. In layout, it resembles a listing presentation and in function it is just like a listing presentation. I go over every page in the booklet, asking questions and getting agreement as I go. At the end is my buyer representation agreement for them to sign so that I am their only agent and can represent them. I also include a pre-application worksheet from my lender in the booklet. I pull the worksheet out and get the buyers on the phone with my lender so they can discuss their financing strategy.

"I'm going to make copies of the agreement you just signed and get the showing sheets for the homes we will see today," is a line that sells every time. They talk in private to the lender, and in 30 minutes I get a call letting me know if I have a live one.

Getting "referability"

Discrimination and referability fit in here also. We all know the law says that we must not discriminate. Even if we didn't have the law, it would still be wrong, as well as bad business. By having a set way every client is handled, I avoid ever having the issue come up. Every client knows that they are seeing an established system—I'm not winging it. Likewise, before a client will refer you they not only need to have been served well, but they need to know that the friend or family member they refer will get the same treatment. My system does that every time, predictably.

We will discuss this screening system in more depth in the next chapter, but now we must move on to selecting the list of homes to show and sell. Never, even in the privacy of your own mind, say, "I'm showing houses." You are "selling houses." No one is served by showing. The roads are wearing out quickly enough without agents driving up and down sight-seeing.

"Satisficing" is my job here. By this point I have a list of needs and wants, an idea of where they need to live, and an opinion about how honest they are with themselves. Generally, any agent who knows how to log into a computer can create a list of houses to show that meets the needs and most of the wants of an average buyer. The trick is to do it for the monthly payment they want or the one the lender says they can make. This is why you can't satisfy anyone. The term "satisfice" means to get close enough to what everyone wants that they can all go along with the decision. House Perfect doesn't exist.

The main players here are Mr. and Ms. Buyer and the lender. Never forget the lender. In fact, let the lender help you.

Position yourself in the dialog so that the lender sets the limits if your buyers are bit too optimistic in pricing. You're wise if you never have to say, "Karen, you can't have that house." Let the lender say it. Once the buyers are realistic in pricing, the list of homes you show them becomes easier to create. And every house on the list will be in their price range. If they want it, they can have it and *they know it*.

This is a key point. Deciding which house to buy is a difficult decision and requires your client's entire attention. If they have some other concern such as "can we afford this" or "will you really get this new job," then making a decision moves from hard to impossible.

Let's take a break to discuss one of the messy details that comes up at about this point. On my initial call to the buyers after they have been referred, or when they called off an ad, I ask a few questions about their needs and wants. Usually they tell me what house payment they would like and enough personal stuff that I can do a search for possible homes. I may do this two days ahead. However, on the day I'm showing the houses, I call every listing agent or at least the listing office to confirm that the place is still on the market. Remember, dear colleague, getting buyers all hyped up to buy a house that is already under contract is no way to win friends and influence people. Now back to the selling sequence.

Why they lie

Why buyers can't tell the truth is the question we are still dealing with. We are getting closer to the answer. Here is how it goes down: I have created the best list of properties to show in the history of real estate sales. I have listened, questioned, pre-qualified (or rather, had the lender pre-qualify), researched, and checked the status. I am ready to ink a deal. Then after the first two houses, I realize they will not like any of the ones I've got today. What happened?

Odds are it is one of only a few things. Often the buyers are trying to buy their parent's home.

"Pam, I want a house just like we had when I was a kid. You know, the big trees and quiet streets. Like over just north of the mall." After two houses you can see their taste is not in line with their emotions. Small, dark houses with small closets and lots of maintenance issues aren't where they are. The closets seemed bigger when they were kids. Usually this dream dies hard. They generally go though a half-day asking why I can't find them a house in this neighborhood with higher ceilings and bigger closets. I could as easily turn lead into gold. You'll see one way to handle this in the We Found It story.

Sometimes we lose time because the client wants to be cool and live where he thinks it sounds good to live. I've seen it take four or five showings to convince a buyer that he did not want a box in a great area, but a nice house in a good area. Sooner or later almost everyone comes to understand that when you drive up to the house at the end of the workday it needs to feel like home. Not a *house* but his *personal place*, the one that makes him feel satisfied, relaxed, and safe. The next issue is—how will we know if they like it?

Books have been written about buyer signs and signals. Zig Ziglar has made a career of it, and some of his books are helpful. For my money, Chapters 10 and 13 in the old classic by Tom

Hopkins, *How to Master the Art of Selling*, say it all on this topic. When you are ready for this book, read it cover to cover. For now, you need to have a few solid clues to work with.

Best buying signal

Taking measurements is the best signal. When the buyers start stepping off where the stereo will go, or better yet where the baby bed will go, it is time to get back to the office and write them up.

Try this dialog: "In a market this hot, we had better do the paperwork on this one to tie it up before someone buys out from under us." It usually works. They will often want to see two more homes after this, but then you need to be heading back to the office.

Sure, the close I gave you is just that, a sales close. But like every truly good close, it is the truth too. If you ever want to feel like a goat in this business, get a young couple all psyched on a house and then go back and tell them it went under contract two hours ago. They will compare each of the next eight (or 80) houses to the one that got away.

Another, more subtle, buying sign is eye contact. The buyers will look at each other if they really like the house. Each wants to know if their partner is on board. When you see the eye contact, it will often be followed by them touching.

On the other hand, when you have shown them a house you thought would answer the mail, pay close attention to how they act when they leave it. If the clients seem to relax as they are leaving, after the decision to move on, instead of the tension of actually making a decision, that's bad. When they change the subject to work or family, or just ask non-emotional questions of each other, you may have a problem.

Occasionally you will get clients who have agreed to some feature or group of features that they think the other one wants and it turns out that neither one wants the stuff. I know it sounds odd, but I have never lost a dime of commission by *underestimating* the amount of coordination and communication a married couple actually does. Just because they live together, they believe they know each other. Another common misperception! After a few days in the car with them, I often feel I know more about the relationship I am observing than the participants do.

Speaking of relationship, I am a service provider. I carry all the expertise and professionalism I can into every transaction. But at the end of the day, I still see people buy the wrong house. I always remind myself that I am someone's mother, but not theirs. During the initial buyer-book presentation I tell every client that if they decide to buy a bad deal, I will explain why it is a bad deal three times and word the warning differently each time. If they still want to do it, I will shut up and take my commission. Usually this does not help, but it makes me feel better. In any case, they always blame the agent. Sometimes they have to.

Out-of-town buyers especially seem to arrive with preconceived ideas and end up with a house that is exactly what they said they wanted and are not happy with it. Knowing what your lifestyle will be in a new house is always difficult. It is even more difficult when the job, the city, the commute, and even the weather are new and different.

Several years ago, I was in a seminar with the owner of a huge nationwide real estate company, and he asked the roomful of 23 very good agents how many inspectors were on the list they give their clients to choose from. (This is for the technical inspection, not the appraisal, which in Texas is usually done during the option period.) The answers ranged from three to "the whole list." I said I only gave buyers one name, and I set the appointment myself. He agreed with me.

His logic was that if anyone makes a mistake in the transaction, the agent will be sued along with everyone else. The agent has insurance and most inspectors don't. For the record, some errors and omissions (E&O) insurers and real estate companies may require that you offer a certain number of inspectors. In this situation, you must get the client to select from and sign a list, which is fine. I would just *check* next to the correct choice. I have a fiduciary duty to guide my clients and I've seen too many deals messed up by incompetent inspectors.

The stories that follow illustrate some of what we have discussed. They are actual events we lived. Because they are real, with only the names and places changed to protect the guilty, they cover more topics than just those we have discussed. Enjoy them and keep them in mind. We now proceed to some of the problem children of the buyer category and how to handle them, stay sane, and still get paid.

We Found "It," Pam!

All buyers know exactly what they want, but sometimes they can't bring it to mind without a bit of help. Usually my system works just fine, and I recommend it to every one of you who has given up a sunny Saturday morning with the kids to show houses to people you just met. Occasionally, clients come along who need a little extra help in the clarification department. These particular guys needed a push, or at least to be sent to the right place.

Mark and Tammy were referred by an acquaintance as a "classic nice young couple." I love a classic. They looked great, and both had winning, vivacious attitudes. We met in the office, as is my habit, and went over the home-buying booklet. I worked up a needs and wants analysis, part of the system. They really wanted out of the apartment (very clear on this) and were in love with the older-style homes they grew up in, the 30-year-old stuff inside the Beltway (not so clear to me).

I made notes and listened, but I had a problem. Their words and lifestyle were not in sync. Maybe I was missing something. A traditional eight-foot-ceiling home with a big yard, big trees, and small, dark rooms with small closets didn't seem right for a young couple that went to the lake every weekend and flew airplanes upside-down for the *fun of it*. Mark actually flew stunt planes, while Tammy liked jet-skiing. Who was going to be interested in the big yard and in maintaining an old money pit of a house? And from the sound of it, I would have bet the farm Tammy had more clothes in her closet than Rich's first wife, who was a genuine prodigy in that respect.

As an agent, I have often found it wise to just listen to clients and do what they asked of me as long as it was not illegal, immoral, or fattening. Just how wise is open to debate.

We spent a Saturday looking at 30-year-old homes that were all too dark, too small, and too cramped (which is client-speak for "you picked some dogs for us to look at.") We were all busy during the next week, so I found them back in my van on Saturday. However, I had developed a Plan B for this excursion. Take it to the bank: spending three hours looking at homes your clients hate is no fun and will never make you any money. You heard it here first!

After viewing two older homes and listening to them howl, I said I needed to drop off a piece of paper at a builder's office. They didn't mind the detour; we were all tired of the old neighborhood. I bought us all a soda on the way to help change mental gears and restore positive attitudes.

The small subdivision that I happened to turn in to would be a short commute for the wife and easily within their budget. Now, as luck would have it, and luck always works better when you plan for it, I parked in front of a new spec home with a big tree and a small yard. The model home was three lots down from this house, so I said I would be a few minutes and said, "Why don't you go have fun in the spec house? I'll be back." The day was warm and the van's air conditioning was off.

When I got to the model home, I introduced myself to the on-site sales representative. This was a different person from the one who had been on duty two days previously when I previewed the area. He asked me what he could do for me, having never seen me before. I said I needed a glass of water and that we had to wait a few minutes so my clients could buy his spec home three doors down.

He gave me a cautious glance and handed me a plastic cup. Most on-site guys consider straight-commission agents an odd bunch. In his experience, agents showed homes rather than dropped clients off in the heat to go into an air-conditioned sales office to wait for them.

Mark and Tammy were smart people and knew what they wanted in their hearts. They just hadn't told their mouths yet. If I had pushed them into the new house, I would have been selling. As it was, they were buying, which is a lot more fun.

In less than 10 minutes, they bounded into the office with large smiles and began telling me about the perfect home they had just "found." I went back with them to ooh and ah and congratulated them on their selection.

From this point on, except for one issue, it was a pretty routine transaction. This was 1997, and I had not heard the question Tammy handed me about financing before. But given her situation, it was perfectly logical. She was one of those fortunate people who had a truly rich dad, which is much less common than the sugared variety. Every spring her trust sent her a check between $10 and $15,000 depending on the stock market. We were closing in early October, so Tammy asked how much the mortgage payment would shrink in January when her money came in and she plunked it into the house. I gave her the textbook answer, the line about paying down the mortgage reducing the time it will take them to pay off the house and saving interest over the long run. Well, this was not the answer Tammy wanted. It was, by the way, always a good idea to give her the answer she wanted (she had a moderate case of Recovering Princess Syndrome).

Her syndrome aside, the question seemed to make sense. Why not get a lower payment if you put in a big chunk of money a few months after closing? This deal became my first split loan. I did not know this term back then, but what we did was a first loan at 80% of the purchase price, a second loan at 15% of the purchase price, and 5% down payment (80/15/5). This got rid of mortgage insurance, which more than made up for the slightly higher interest rate on the second loan. It also gave Tammy what she wanted. In January she could pay off the second loan and the payment would reduce without the expense of refinancing. It also had an immediate advantage to these clients. They were both working, with no children and no deductions, so converting the price of the mortgage insurance, which is not deductible on income taxes, to mortgage interest charges, which are, saved them money from month one.

Nowadays, split loans with 80% first mortgages and 15% or 10% seconds are very common. And because Tammy wanted something special, I started using them before most agents in central Texas found out they were available. What she wanted also fit my basic criteria: not illegal, immoral, or fattening.

A client's perceptions are not always wrong, nor will they always let go of them when confronted with obvious contradictions. However, treating intelligent people intelligently usually helps. In any case, I'm an agent, not a therapist. The art is in figuring out which part of the client's wishes are real. Putting a little thought into what these fine people wanted made this deal happen. They have continued to reward us with repeat business and referrals for almost a decade.

༄

This next story has a few twists and turns and did not end as well as it should have. Rich had the fun of actually handling these showings.

Finding a Home for a Bear

As I am well into my second half-decade as a full-time agent, I can say without fear of contraception that I've found a lot of different types of houses for various sorts of people. Log houses, energy-efficient houses, frame houses, ranch houses, big ones, little ones: I've sold them all. I've sold them to Christians, Muslims, gays, women, men, trusts, and others, but two years ago a couple was referred to me who had a stuffed bear. Not being a person to get excited over details, I noted this on my call log and coordinated their arrival date from Alaska. (Alaska? There was a hint here, but I missed it.)

I was excited about this lead because the people who referred them were nice people whom I had just helped buy their new house. The deal had its problems, but the people were great (see the story You Can Get Bit in Chapter 3). This great truism in real estate is *usually* true: nice people refer nice people. These new clients seemed to be good folks on the phone, and are friends of ours to this day.

Their Air Alaska plane arrived and the new folks, Paul and Windy, were in the office going through the system and doing the final needs analysis within 90 minutes of landing. They wanted to start the house hunt.

The bear issue came up again, only this time I stopped to ask a question, "Why the big deal about the bear? Can't you just put it in the living room?" They were taking this bear issue way too seriously, in my opinion. Not three months before, we had sold a house for a chemical-plant designer who had 32 mounted trophies. Since he was in South America leveling a forest to build a refinery, I had to supervise packing and shipping this fauna to the new house in Louisiana. It was an aggravation, but a lot of things are.

I had selected a number of homes that had two large living areas; no problem—one for them to live in, and one to be a trophy room for the dead animals. Generally, hunters don't have just one stuffed creature, they own a variety. I confidently pulled out the pile of perfect home listings I had selected to show them. I felt I had this under control.

Then they showed me the picture.

This was not a bear, it was a beast. It was mounted on its hind legs, mouth open—the normal bear pose you see in all the movies. But this thing was over nine feet tall and standing on a 12-inch platform, which was clearly needed to hold the weight.

We are talking about a creature towering two feet over Tim Duncan or Wilt Chamberlain. Alive, this guy weighed 1,200 pounds. In the back of my mind, I remembered having seen a nature movie where a bear kills a full-grown bull moose out of hand. But in the movies, they just picture the bear and moose; the trees looked a bit small, but the size of the animals did not come through. The reality of size does not hit you until you see the six-foot-tall man, the big guy at the table with you, in the picture—and his head doesn't reach the magnificent creature's armpit.

This great furry thing had too much emotional presence for me to let in my house if it paid rent, but Paul and Windy seemed to like it. Just to keep it interesting, they also wanted to be allowed to park their 22-foot boat on the property. (Repeat to yourself "the client is always right" 100 times quickly.)

The home search took on a different aspect.

In the $160,000 to $200,000 price range in San Antonio, homes were available that will allow the display of this sort of trophy in communities with very flexible home-owner's associations. And I found them. However, each house had something just a little bit wrong with it. At times I can be a bit slow on the uptake, but eventually I get it. After the fourth or fifth perfect house, I started to watch the eyes. The large living rooms in houses that you could park a boat next to were not moving *her*. Well guess what, my dear colleague: 95% of the time *he* does not buy a house that *she* does not want to live in. I don't care how tall his trophy, what size his boat, or how big his guns: the first rule of home buying is *the wife must think it is home*. This one was not interested in sleeping in a museum, but she did not know this about herself clearly enough to put it into words.

She loved her husband and wanted him to be happy. But I just don't think she wanted a bear for a roommate. Of course I'm only guessing about the bear. But here is a fact you can take to the bank: a woman can find a good reason not to buy a house if she feels she needs to. In retrospect the signs were all there. They had not been looking at each other when discussing the houses. In fact, they seemed to part company inside them and each do their own thing. Windy had explained a lot about life in Alaska as we drove around, but asked few questions about the houses we were looking at. Paul kept wanting to tell me about bear hunting, and I kept avoiding it.

Realizing I had wasted a day and a half, I did a course correction and showed them an absolutely clean two-year-old home in a gated community, and that was that. The house was the exact commuting distance they wanted, near the stores they wanted to be near, and met all the rest of their priorities except for the bear and boat. It was a sweet deal and an easy closing.

Now to be fair, they had to look at the bigger homes to get an understanding of what they wanted, or in this case what they didn't want. I think we are all born with opinions just like we are born with navels. We simply get them confused. Because we all know where our navel is, we think we should know where our opinion is also. Of course life does not work that way. Some people spend months figuring it out.

In fact, this story does not even end with this purchase. Their self-exploration continued until they saw *past the features.*

One of the biggest problems buyers have is that they get all wrapped up on a feature that they think will make their life unique, or cool, or complete. At the end of the day, no such feature exists. The real issues, the mega-issues, are values and lifestyle. The place for the bear, the easy commute, even the clean house were not really where these people were. They were, and are, individualists. They love to see trees, to have some privacy, and to be able to go to the coast or lake or deer lease and have some fun. I think Paul would sit on his back porch in his underwear if he could.

At the time we were looking for the house, they were adamant about the commute and being close to stores and other secondary things. I suppose they had been told these were things to look for in a good purchase, and everyone wants to be cool and make a good purchase. Now that they have made a good purchase, what they really want is a house on three acres and trees, even if it were 15 or 20 miles from work and with no store within 10 miles.

This is not a sad ending for them. They inherited 20 acres in Florida near an Air Force base that they can transfer to in the near future; both are civil-servant types. Finally, they will have the right home.

I don't have a solution to avoiding this problem in the first place. When I meet new people, I try to get them to let me select a variety of homes in different neighborhoods, at different price ranges, so that they can see the options. It is part of the system. But too often the clients let opinion rule and will block out even looking at what may interest them.

One of the oldest and least true statements in real estate is "buyers are liars." This is not the case. It is just that old "navel versus opinion" issue coming into play.

About the bear, I have never seen it. It is currently in a small museum in Alaska, where I am sure it is well cared for and appreciated. The boat was sold to a sportsman in Alaska who needed the monster for the big water of the North Pacific. A smaller one was purchased here and lives in Corpus Christi, where boats should live. Our clients hunt or fish almost every weekend and remain committed to enjoying as much of life as they can. It's funny; I spent 22 years as an Army officer, but can't bring myself to ask how that beautiful beast was killed.

03

Rich handled these next buyers too, lucky man. You can tell they made an impression on him. In fact, he has a whole new concept of the term "litter box." For our purposes, you will see that we just did not appreciate what our needs analysis really meant. We all know about neighborhood covenants, but when working with buyers who have an odd hobby or a special need, the word is "disclose, disclose, disclose."

You Have To Ask

We are cat lovers and usually have at least two adorable Siamese cats living with us. Well, usually adorable; no Siamese male is *always* anything, and against that standard, Sebastian does not appear singular. After a hard day of napping, he can be depended on to take a chunk out of any guest overstaying *his* welcome. Owing to circumstance, bad planning, and inattention to detail, we've had as many as four cats at one time, but we are the original pikers compared to this buyer couple. Can you imagine having 14 cats voluntarily? The number tends to fluctuate as they find strays that need homes and then find homes for others, but 14 is reasonably average for their place.

Now, if a person has 14 cats in the house any knowledgeable observer would concede that the cats will cause some issues. In fact, they could change a person's life, outlook on the world, hope of salvation, and political affiliation. That they would have a major impact on being able to buy a home is not so obvious. Of course, the real issue for home buying is not the cats but rather organizational mindsets. The organization in this case is the neighborhood home-owner's association, affectionately known as the HOA. These, like the neighborhoods and people they represent, come in all sizes and outlooks. Most are necessary and even reasonable, but not all. In older areas, many HOAs are run by the old-line residents for the benefit of the past. They know how things should be done, always have been done, and always will be done. I think in their less lucid moments the Stalag 5 syndrome sets in. This is a form of group think that causes ordinarily nice people to feel the need to wear brown shirts and sing in beer halls while trying to run other people's lives. On more than one occasion, when negotiating for a client, I have wanted to remind the HOA president that the Fuhrer was dead and his fan club disbanded.

The other problem-type of HOA is the new home community. The builder still owns the HOA and will keep control until he completes construction, and he knows exactly how to do this. He hires an attorney.

Here, the difficulty for rational minds is the Model Home hang-up. This is not actually a mindset in the strictest sense; that would imply a personality. We are agents, and no agent I have ever met thinks that builders have much in the way of personality; therefore, how could they have a personality problem? What substitutes for personality is habit. His Holiness in Rome, a person who has not changed tailors in 900 years, is radical compared to the conservatism of the average builder. This is not just sour grapes from the guy the builder does not want to pay a 3% commission to when he is already making 20% on the deal. I'm talking existential reality.

Here is a great example of this habitual caution: For 20 years we have had technologies for home construction that cut utility costs over 60% per annum and builders will not use them, because they are "too new." Saving a home buyer $100 a month on electric bills is just not worth taking a risk. Well, they don't take risks with HOAs either. Their goal is to have every home look like a model home until they build the last house and leave. They will restrict the type of fence their members can have, the color of the front door, and the number of pets. I believe they would restrict the numbers of kids that clients could have if the government would let them.

We can return to the story now; I just needed to vent.

Unaccompanied by his wife, Bob was having a new home built in a lovely neighborhood in Schertz, a small suburb on the northeast side of San Antonio. His wife had sent him to town to purchase the home (but that's another story!). After a couple days of working out the deal and arranging financing, we were ready to select colors before he got on a plane for home in two days. During the two-hour process of selecting the finish-out colors and fixtures, our talkative buyer mentioned to the salesperson that he wanted beige tile downstairs "for the cats."

"Oh, really," the timid salesman interjected. "You have cats?" (pregnant pause) "How many?"

They seemed innocent-enough questions. Once the answer "just fourteen" hit the airwaves, though, the salesperson's whole attitude changed, along with his color. He was new with this company and sales were slow. He needed our cat-loving client, or at least this sale, and here was a deal killer.

It turns out no more than two pets per home were allowed in this neighborhood. Now that he knew how many cats the client had, the salesperson had to withdraw the purchase contract or notify the home-owner's association of the violation even before the client had the home built, much less took possession.

In the one- to four-family residential contract in Texas, there is a great line that most people don't know how to use. It is in Paragraph 6 along with the survey, in Section D, to be specific. It reads:

> D. OBJECTIONS: Within ___ days after Buyer receives the Commitment, Exception Documents and the survey, Buyer may object in writing to defects, exceptions, or encumbrances to title: disclosed on the survey other than items 6A(1) through (7) above; disclosed in the Commitment other than items 6A(1) through (8) above; or which prohibit the following use or activity:_____.

For reasons known only to the real estate gods, most people write "residential" on that line. Now, if you are not allowed to use a property for residential use, why are you using the one- to four-family *residential* contract? Actually, this is the place to write in anything that would cause the buyer to *not buy the house if they're not allowed to do it*—such as have 14 cats, park an RV on the grass, sit in skivvies on the back porch, or put a bear in the parlor. This paragraph puts everyone on notice that, "If objections are not cured within such 15 day period, this contract will terminate and the earnest money will be refunded to Buyer unless Buyer waives the objections."

Unfortunately, this paragraph is not a part of any new home contract, so that was not an option. The buyer was not trying to hide anything; the topic of 14 cats just hadn't come up, but neither had his blood type or preference in whisky. Remember, the builder has the attorney and gets to write his own contract. If Paragraph 6 had been available, I would have used it. This is not what the builder wants.

A builder is fundamentally different from an average seller who has one house to sell and only succeeds if the deal closes. The builder doesn't really care if something comes up during construction that kills the deal. Remember, the builder wants to build. When a qualified buyer signs a construction contract, the builder can get what is known as interim financing. Or to put it more clearly, the builder gets to use the client's credit to get money to build a house. Often he has used his own up to the limit. If the client finds out that something is amiss in the house, the neighborhood, or the quality of the house and jumps ship, the builder still gets to build the house. What is the bank going to do when half the interim financing is already spent on construction? In the trade we call this a spec (built on speculation) house; the builder calls it a gift.

Our tale has a happy ending. We were able to find a beautiful home in a neighborhood where the client and his 14 cats can live in peace. It has a very high fence and a ton of tile. For me, the best part was that this home was a few years old and a better buy than the new home, as they usually are. The buyers were military and will need to get some appreciation before their next move.

HOAs can be fun but usually aren't. Also, builders will tell you the bottom line, but only if you ask.

ଓ

2 Great Models Beat Great Brains

Or, Only Action Counts

Have you ever noticed that some business people do not seem to have the problems most of us have? They appear to make money with less effort and have more fun. It could be that they are just smarter, but I doubt that and so do you. The world is cluttered with smart guys that don't have a nickel.

I think it is because of systems.

A few years ago, Rich and I had breakfast with another husband and wife team. This couple sold over 50 million dollars' worth of houses the previous year, they own a bunch of real estate offices, and the husband is a significant real estate investor. That is what we wanted to discuss. It is one thing to make money, but money isn't wealth until it comes from an investment. The conversation went something like this:

"Jim, you always seem to get good appreciation; how do you select what to buy?" Jim opened his planner and pulled out a sheet of paper. On half the sheet was printed the criteria that he used.

"When I find one that meets my profile, Pam, I buy it."

Good models equal good profit

No agonizing, no reflecting, just action. Their rental portfolio was producing $26,000 a month positive cash flow then. By now, they are making some real money. What is most interesting to us about the model, and Rich still has that piece of paper, is its conservative simplicity. My point is that it may not be the best model, but it works and it is used every time. That is where the strength is. Jim did not know Pam was going to ask this question; he just keeps his models handy. Long ago I found out that Jim can go to any dry-erase board and lay out his entire business plan from memory and put in current numbers on the economic model. One criterion of The Business Owner Mindset is to have a passion for really knowing the critical details of your business. This couple could be poster children for the BOM.

As an agent, you can spend a lot of time worrying about a client's ability to get a loan, his or her commitment to buy, and their urgency to buy. You can't afford the time or gas to show someone 20 houses only to find out he doesn't qualify for a loan, or is in a lease for seven more months.

The answer is to let the system work for you.

When I get three new agents together I can count on six reasons why an agent can't get a buyer representation commitment signed at the first client meeting. Here is the secret: the first meeting is the *easiest* time to get it signed. Clients sign something at the dentist's office before their teeth get cleaned. Buying a house is at least that big a deal.

The next responsibility shuffle agents do is to give clients a list of three or five lenders to call and "check rates" or "see which one you like." Steering is the excuse and to "avoid liability." I think they are not sure enough of their process knowledge and they lack confidence to explain it. Both of these are really simple to clients. They can't get market information and see homes without the agent, and it does not do a lot of good to find a home to buy if they don't have a loan lined up. This is complicated? Why not just say this to the clients?

There is a secret about home loans that agents do not appreciate. Almost all loans to creditworthy clients are "conforming" loans. What one broker has, the next one will have, or one about as good. The lenders themselves are the big difference. Some close deals on time and at the fees and rates they quoted the client, and others play games with the client's money. My job is to know a good one and get my clients to that lender. I do this in the most straightforward manner I can think of. See what you think of this approach:

"Mr. Buyer, do have a lender you know and trust to do your loan?" Typically, the answer is no.

"This is a pre-application worksheet my lender uses; while I'm making copies I want you to discuss mortgage strategies with her." I dial the number, say hi to the lender, hand over the phone and head for the copier with my signed representation form.

Let clients de-select

Sometimes a person will not want to sign the buyer rep agreement after my buyer-book presentation and will not want to let the lender "pull credit." When this happens, I see it as a positive event. Without this information I can't evaluate the client. If I haven't developed enough trust for the client to commit to letting me represent them, then we have a problem. Quite possibly I don't need to spend time with this person because *they are not ready to be a client*. At this point I have only invested about 30 minutes of time and no gas. If they wish to "de-select" themselves from my schedule, now is the time.

Rich and I spend a lot of time evaluating our presentations. We know that the system is key to a productive business. What we do is standardized. We seldom skip any steps. When we do, we always pay for it in time, money, or both.

A committed client wants to do the job right. They do not know how much house they can afford, they don't know the process, and most of all they don't want surprises. Remember they are in fear at this moment. As they see the process more clearly, they begin to see me as a consultant, not a salesperson. I present options; they make educated selections. People who don't want this sort of guidance, who just want to drive around and see if something strikes their fancy, don't need to be in my car—or yours either.

Options need a little more explanation.

Selecting the homes to put before a client requires more than a little judgment and a lot of market knowledge. Remember Mark and Tammy? After I had gotten to know them and had a clear concept of how to manage them, I selected a particular home to put in front of them. Of course, leaving them in a hot car in front of the air-conditioned spec house was a bit overt; but, subtleness is overrated and has never been my strong point. You shouldn't worry about it either.

Choosing the correct properties is something to worry over. At any given time, there are probably 100 homes an average buyer could consider in the San Antonio metro area that generally meet the client's criteria. That's nice to know, but I have dropped the ball if I have to show ten homes before writing an offer. If I have listened to the clients as we do the needs analysis, watched their reaction to the first few homes I show them, and caught the meaning of the comments they made in the car between showings, I should know what they want. At this point, don't stand on ego. Get effective.

Show the right houses

Guessing is only acceptable at the beginning. More than once, I have asked clients to finish their sodas in the waiting room and gone back to set new showing appointments. If I missed a key factor earlier and don't feel good about the homes I've scheduled, *I don't show them.* It's that simple. Looking smooth in front of a client is not nearly as important as showing good stuff. The issue is my credibility, and this is a two-sided issue. How can I sell something I don't think is what the client wants? The other side is that the client knows if you have heard them. They don't give any atta-boys for driving them around for three hours on a hot day looking at houses they aren't interested in. Remember, I want to "get it right," not "be right," because closed deals trump looking cool any day.

I hope this has sounded simple so far, because now we will get into the weeds a bit. In one of the stories at the end of this chapter, the issue of the clients' criteria gets very confusing. The clients, grandparents of local residents, were moving to town because the missus's new job was all traveling and online. They could live anywhere they wanted, so why not live close to the kids? As we went about looking at homes with the clients, the adult daughter and the three grandkids, I started wondering who the decision maker was. What factors were influencing the decision? The clients were old farm folks who said they wanted to be close to town, but in an area with a "country feel." The grandchildren wanted a pool to use after school, and the daughter had child-care issues.

The story will explain the tale, but for now I want you to consider that the other person in the car, the 35-year-old daughter in this case, may steer or even control the decision. Here, the daughter was determined to have Mom and Dad close by to help with the three kids. A single mom can be persistent. After a half day wasted, I figured out the clients were saying what they thought they wanted (country, with a large lot), but actually their heart was with their daughter and grandkids. It took hours for their heart to tell their mouth what to say.

Once I got the message I focused the search and sold a house. In the three stories in this section I have shown variations on this idea. It happens all the time. Once you really understand the motivation, take them to the right property and let them buy it.

Don't over-show

Oversell and confusion are the biggest enemies at this point. When you know what they want, show them a great house that works for them. When showing this house, don't talk more than you need in order to explain features or discuss condition. You know it is the right house, but you have to let them discover it. Do not show them three more just as good and confuse the issue. Normally people will want to see two more houses after they see the right one. I suppose they just feel obligated to not miss anything.

Your gut will tell you the best house for a particular client; in the case of the grandparents we discussed above, I felt they only had one real option to select. If you are going to show five houses to a client, put the best one at number three. This lets the clients evaluate the good one against the first two and compare it to the next two. They get to *buy* the house with this sequence rather than feel they have been *sold*.

Your confidence is key at this point. I have a contract already filled out except for the particulars of the address and price. Mentally, I am ready to write up the deal and I know I won't forget any details particular to this specific client. My preparation, and the confidence it gives me, allows me to focus on the key issues that will get a sale closed: listening to the clients and using the most effective dialogs. I want my clients to commit to the purchase and their future, and take the house off the market before someone else gets it.

As you read the next few stories, consider what we have discussed.

Who Else is in the Back Seat?

Pat called with another referral. The parents of the nice girl across the street were moving to town and needed a house. I made the calls, sent the emails, researched, emailed pictures of houses, chatted up the daughter (Jeanie for future reference), and all the usual stuff. When clients are only going to be in town for a few days, I like to be ready for them. Given that buyers don't know what they want, it is always good to have a plan so you can change it. When I call clients, especially out-of-town ones, I ask open-ended questions, those you can't answer with a yes or no and let them ramble. Everyone has a story, and if they think you are interested they will tell it. If you want a person to think you are a great conversationalist, just listen to them and ask questions. Guaranteed: they will think you're a genius.

If you take the client's list of needs and wants, it should reflect their personality and lifestyle. After they tell me their story, I have a picture of what they actually need in the way of real estate. Kathy is talkative and I got their whole life history. It did not work as expected in this instance, but the technique is worth knowing. And their story was classic Americana.

Kathy and Leonard were a prototypical early-70s couple. Leonard had been a real live farmer in the Midwest until the Reagan bust of the late 80s broke his credit and he literally lost the farm, as Leonard put it. They really stopped having fun for a while when his heartbeat started changing quicker than the stock market and he had his first bypass surgery. This part of their history ended up with a silver lining, or at least an aluminum one.

Kathy got into the health-care industry and moved up quickly. She was a natural for the business and believed in the old adage, "if you can't beat them, join them." This is why they were coming to San Antonio.

She had reached a level that caused her to travel so much it did not matter where they lived. That being the case, they did what comes naturally these days for people that don't have the farm anymore. They were moving to the grandkids. As far as a features list goes, theirs was short. Just a nice place in the country that was a reasonable commute to the grandchildren and not too far from a hospital. Kathy didn't trust the old man's ticker enough for real rural living anymore.

I should have picked up on something when Jeanie and the two youngest came with Mom and Dad to look at houses. It is not uncommon for a parent or grown child to come along and see the houses. But when they do it with young kids, something is up. "Another set of eyes doesn't hurt," was the way I inappropriately glossed over it.

I did not get Jeanie's story until later. She had just been through an amiable divorce. That is one where one partner concedes anything the other asks to untie the marriage knot. The usual reason the filing party concedes so much is that the relationship isn't going anywhere and he needs his space. This generally means the space he is looking for is the area next to his girlfriend. The ex-wife can even have custody of the three kids, except on weekends when the weather is nice. She'd had a usual divorce. As the reality of single parenthood settled in on this astute lady, she felt a growing need for *help*.

Wish I hadn't missed this up front.

I covered the buyer-book presentation and confirmed the needs and wants list before we left. Jeanie's only interjection was that it needed to have a pool and be within walking distance of her house. We all laughed and headed for my van. The theme music from *Jaws* should have been playing in the background.

I spent a day showing, not selling, beautiful homes in the

hills just north of town. All were easy commutes to Jeanie's house and she said she was happy about the locations. But (dear reader, you knew a but was coming), she seemed to plant a poison pill in every one of them. "Too many steps out the back door," or "Is that water damage?" and "That is an ugly color; I wonder how many coats it will take to cover it?"

It went on like this all day. She was congenial, but just kept at it. When a sharp person gets focused they can be effective. She knew the poison pill technique so well I would not have bought an apple from her, even though I'm not the fairest in the land.

One of the kids had an afternoon soccer game, so, mercifully, we had to finish early. On the way back to the office, I fished around for what Jeanie wanted. She gave me some neighborhoods she knew her parents would love.

Not a lot of real estate was for sale in the areas she gave me, but they were all in cycling distance from her house. Why didn't I know that was coming? I called Jeanie that night.

"Houston, we have a problem."

She had me believing she would kill everything I had to show if it didn't meet *her* needs. The problem was that where she wanted her folks to live did not have anything suitable on the market. Worse than this, I had come to realize that Leonard and Kathy had talked about country because they thought it was what they should want. At the end of the day, they wanted the grandkids to bike over to their house as much as Jeanie needed them to. I decided to get concerned and moved "pool" from the want to the need list.

The next day I dug out the best of a mediocre bunch to show Leonard and Kathy and called Jeanie again to see if she had any great ideas. I wanted to be helpful, but I'm only human.

Why not share the monkey she was trying to put on my back? Fair is fair. However, before I could even get smug, much less express it, she had an address for me. The previous night Jeanie had called her contact list, a sort of housewife underground network. One of the neighbors four blocks away was selling his house, but it was not listed yet.

I called the clients and postponed our morning appointment and delayed the showing times on the homes I had set. The direct approach was necessary. After a few minutes of research I found the owner's name, a Mr. Brackford, and his business number. Before contacting him I drove by the property. Jeanie said he was fixing it up, and if that were true I could probably get in. As I pulled up I noticed the painter's trucks, and knew I had guessed right. What a mess. Painters were hard at work in three different rooms and all the doors and windows were open. The house was perfect. It even had a pool!

I cancelled all the other showings.

Brackford was at his office paying bills. I set an appointment for 20 minutes later. Next, I ran a quick market analysis and grabbed a One Time Showing Agreement. I wanted to know if this guy was realistic on price, and I wanted to demonstrate that I knew what I was talking about. From his tone, the owner sounded like a typical bottom-line-oriented businessperson and was bound to want to talk numbers.

After 30 minutes of discussing all the previous sales he knew about and several he did not know about, I had his confidence. He agreed to let me show the house if I would agree to only a 3% commission if my clients bought it. He had a friend that was going to list it for him, but if I brought him an acceptable offer he would deal with me. We discussed price a bit and I felt he would be reasonable. I needed him to be reasonable because I knew what would happen when Leonard and Kathy saw this one. I could already see the kids jumping in the pool.

Having lived for years on a farm, my clients did not mind stepping over paint cans and walking on drop cloths. They saw what I had seen earlier. This one was the house they described in the location Jeanie had demanded. I now had "sold" buyers on an unlisted house and the only document I had was a "One Time Showing Agreement." And we had just used it. This place even had built-in kid beds and a loft in one bedroom. If I didn't get this house, my chances of finding one just as good were next to nothing.

I hate not having a Plan B.

We wrote up the offer immediately and I went back to Brackford's office. As it turned out, he was a true business man and in a dealing mood. I agreed to accept my commission and treat him fairly. He agreed to my estimation of value.

The rest of the story was routine.

The buyers appreciated that I listened and tried to help. They were impressed that I would go to the owner's business on a Sunday afternoon and negotiate their contract. The owner was impressed, too. When the buyers, Jeanie, and Brackford teamed up to send us four referrals during the next nine months, we were impressed. Brackford even referred a listing to us before we closed the deal on his house: Dr. H, the dentist, and now our dentist.

༄

This next tale is a celebration of the fact that intellect, the kind measured on IQ tests, doesn't do much for you in real estate. Between Dr. D and his wife, they had six college degrees and two brilliant minds. Both were published scholars and out to lunch on how to deal with home buying.

Having to Rent is a State of Mind

"They were all thugs," Dr. D said in the middle of a discussion of Frankish monarchs (These are the seventh-century guys who ran most of France, and in fact made it French.) The documentation was pretty substantial that King Clovis, the greatest king of the Franks had lined up his army and raiding buddies for an inspection. "Army" and "raiding buddies" were more or less synonymous.

He walked down the line of warriors and checked each one. When he came to a certain guy, Cragburt by name, the king swung his battle-axe and split the man down the middle to about the sword belt. It turns out that Cragburt had stolen a sacred vessel, a large silver cup, from a church loyal to the king. Cragburt had made it worse by not mentioning the theft to the king before the bishop did, thereby embarrassing King Clovis.

The brutality of the king doing this sort of nasty and very public murder seemed astounding to me, but Dr. D reminded me that history is the study of how "they thought." This was a graduate course and we were all practicing to be professionals.

As you can tell, I never did become a professional historian. I did, however, get the idea that my perceptions can limit both my understanding and ability to see the possibilities of a situation. King Clovis was not particularly interested in the silver cup or the guy who stole it. He was interested in *staying in charge*. If he, the head thug, let a lesser thug get over on him in this little issue, it would only be a matter of time before this or some other miscreant would be splitting the king.

A few weeks later Dr. D. and I had a discussion about houses that demonstrated that the teacher should listen to himself.

Dr. D was the smartest instructor I had in my history masters-degree program and a real inspiration. But he had rented the same house for 13 years. Being a subtle sort of person, I said, "What! You've rented a house for thirteen years; that's crazy!"

"Well yes, Rich, but owning a home is expensive and a big responsibility," was his somewhat sheepish response.

I got myself under control. The thought of this smart guy paying his landlord's mortgage just floored me. I next repressed the fleeting thought that I could buy a nice place and get him for a tenant. (P.T. Barnum is usually credited with saying, "There's a sucker born every minute," and I had a live one in front of me.)

Once I got him over the perception issues, Dr. D and his wife looked at the numbers and realized they were already making a house payment— for a much nicer house than the rundown dog they were renting. Within a week they had bought a new, to-be-built home. The idea that they could live someplace where they could pick out the colors and put art on the walls wowed them. They read dozens of books a year, but no financial pages.

As it turned out, his landlady had a few perception challenges herself. The building process took several months and when it was appropriate, I reminded Dr. D to give his notice to his landlady. Some things must be done by the book, and terminating a lease is one of them. The resulting call I got from Brangana, the Hun landlady, was a hoot. She proceeded to chew me up one side and down the other. How dare I ruin her relationship with good clients, and didn't I know that she was going to keep their deposit because the whole house needed paint and carpet?

I suggested that since she had not painted or carpeted the place in 13 years, nor had she followed appropriate procedures as a landlord, she had better hope I let her off lightly. I would not recommend to Dr. D that he write letters to certain state and local offices complaining of landlord's failure to maintain the property if the entire deposit were returned at move-out. My client got his money.

Dr. D's financial perceptions had been gotten honestly. He had come to America as young man from Corsica and rented in New York City while he learned English, Latin, and Medieval Latin to go with his Italian, French, and Old French. Along the way he got a degree in history before moving to San Francisco. He did his graduate studies at Berkeley.

Neither place lets moderate-income people buy nice houses. To get the house he got here, two miles from the university, would cost $350,000 to $450,000 in San Francisco. He was not in the Bay Area anymore, but his perception was.

சு

These highly educated clients found our buyer presentation just as helpful as first-time homebuyers with high school diplomas do. Good systems are good because they work. Occasionally a situation causes problems, and location is one of the most difficult. The buyer in the next story was a bit unusual because he was not buying an investment property, but he wasn't going to live in it either. He wasn't even in the country.

Two for the Price of One
Or, Who's Your Daddy?

The voice on the phone was pure beauty shop. Beauty shops are unique places in many ways I'm sure, but one factor that is seldom replicated, thankfully, is the tone of the banter. Now I'm not talking about all beauty shops, just the little neighborhood strip-center type.

The upper crust is different. At a recent convention in Las Vegas, Pam decided to get her hair done and I went along for the walk. The shop, if you could call such a facility by so dismissive a term as "shop," was in the resort and looked like architectural art. On the video screen was the corporate founder, a young guy with hair to his waist wearing a black hat and coat, doing a girl's hair over and over with DVD perfection. This place did not have the banter I'm talking about. In fact, it did not have any banter at all; it seemed they were getting ready for communion or a wine tasting. But the voice on the phone reminded me of the strip center and it was more interesting than any DVD. It was a lead.

Jerri had been referred by one of her clients and said she needed to buy two houses and wanted to meet me. Of course someone who needs two houses is always easy to schedule in. Two days later, an early-twenty-something with purple hair swished into the office in a cloud of chatter and a crinkle of plastic. From a great many comments and stories, I pieced together that her dad wanted to help her and her married brother buy houses. The catch was her dad lived in England and only came to the U.S. under duress, claiming a love of civility, but more probably because of the strictures of his second wife.

We called England and got the process explained as well as

was practical and showed the kids some houses. The interesting thing about this process, and the only point that makes this story interesting, was the buyer's awareness of what he wanted.

Working out the features was easy. The kids were broke and neither could balance a checkbook, but they were not hard to please. Dad did not seem difficult either, except that he couldn't bring himself to agree to the first couple of houses I recommended to him. Then I had a thought. His kids were as different as daylight and darkness. One was a purple-headed, bubbly, single-mom beautician; the other was a born-again, married father earning minimum wage. Neither one could really take care of him- or herself in his mind. Actually, they were competent; just young and in the midst of making youthful mistakes. Dad thought they should help each other, but did not know how to express this to me. From experience he knew the concept would be incomprehensible to them.

I found two houses for sale on the same street two blocks apart and emailed him the offer. He sent the earnest money by overnight mail. Dad thought I had a great idea, and I don't think he ever realized that it was what he had in mind the whole time. Being an absentee father for most of the kid's lives, he was justifiably cautious about trying to be authoritarian to them. As much as the kids wanted out of apartments, they could not accept him bullying them. But he was all over the idea that I should be the one to be forceful, opinionated, and authoritative.

A word of caution here about out-of-country deals: little details will cost you days. The son was going to get power of attorney from dad to sign the closing documents so as not to have to mail them to England. However, we did not realize that the closest notary public was 68 miles away from Dad in another city and he had to have an *appointment* to see the guy! This would take days. I had let this detail wait until the last minute, because it did not cross my mind that finding a notary could be an issue. In the U.S. there's a notary under every rock. We overnighted the documents to England and Dad's attorney helped him. In England, notary stamps are hard to come by, but they have as many lawyers as pubs.

I am always fascinated with the different ways in which various cultures look at the same situation. In a world of Enrons and Worldcoms, it was good to see the more rigorous standards of the past on our trip to England. I don't think Henry VII would have allowed a corporate CEO to testify under oath that he did not know how his company was doing financially.

A couple of years ago, Rich and I went back to London. It had been 10 years since we had been there. Touring Westminster Cathedral again, we took a tour that was more detailed than the one we had gone on before. We got to see the old official part of the place, up the dank circular stairs and down the dark hall.

It seems the English government was run out of the Cathedral and the rectory across the street during the early Renaissance. This was just after the king stopped carrying the treasury around with him in strongboxes on wagons. The hall was a uniform gray and not all that well lit, but we got to look into the places where clerks had clerked for time out of mind. In this drabness, I noticed a dirty little thing that looked like leather, maybe part of a shoe, nailed to the door in an old office. This gray, damp-feeling office had to have been important, given that it was cordoned off with velvet ropes, labeled with brass placards, and still had original furnishings. Always the history trivia type, Rich said that the leather thing was a hand. King Henry the VII had caught his notary approving forged contracts and had his hand cut off. The king then had the hand nailed to the door as an integrity reminder to future notaries. Rich had read the story as an undergraduate and was impressed the hand was still there. The nailing had occurred decades before any Englishman had walked in America and no one had ever thought to take the nasty thing down. Rich loved it.

CB

3 Picking Keepers

Or, Don't Let a Few Disasters Hold You Back

Dan and Lisa had just moved to town from Texas's next-favorite state, Mississippi. We like this state not because it's so great, but for just the opposite reason. If it weren't for Mississippi, we would be the worst state in most human services categories: you know, things like health care, education spending, and teacher-student ratios. But we can count on Ole Miss to grab that bottom spot in spite of the best efforts of the Texas biennial Austin Circus and Pep show, often referred to as the legislature in newspaper accounts. I don't mean to be hard on the open collar set that has supported Schultz's Beer Garden for almost a hundred years, but if the shoe fits.... However, they routinely do what the state Board of Realtors tells them to do, except when bankers and big insurance companies lean on them first. I suppose they can't be all bad.

Anyway, Dan and Lisa and their three little kids showed up wanting to own a home and needing a place to stay. These were nice people. I don't just mean okay, I mean special. The smiles, the candor, the openness, not to mention the well-mannered kids who clearly loved and respected their parents: they were the all-American package. We were new agents at the time and made a bunch of calls trying to find a way to help them. But with weak credit, a brand-new job, and little income from that job, they were not getting a mortgage. Being nice, honest, and hard-working does not mean you finish first or even finish at all. (Still, it counts in our minds.)

Attitude is a key part of any successful business. Ours is to keep people who demonstrate integrity, and drop losers. Rich found Dan and Lisa a decent rental and we put them on our newly created mailing list. Good people and great clients don't grow on trees. They were already good people and when they got successful, we would be there to make them great clients.

Screening clients is panning for gold

Dropping losers and keeping winners sounds great, but how do you do it? First, use a system to screen for you. After we developed the buyer-book presentation and required a buyer representation agreement and loan pre-qualification up front, the time spent on Dan and Lisa-s dropped from hours to minutes. Up front we now know who is a high-probability client. Another benefit of a systematic approach is its consistency. By doing the same process with everybody we can demonstrate that we don't discriminate and that we are fair. Of course our system is not perfect—none of them are—but when you pan for gold you have to wash out the rocks.

I still have to listen to the client's story, ask the probing questions, sit back, and let them talk for a while. I want to get a feel for who I'm talking to. Are they honest? Are they candid? Is there something odd in the story? Will they make a commitment to us? The loyal, honest guys with a few challenges in credit history or income are often great to work with and good referral sources. On the other hand, some upper-income types have mental baggage that precludes them from being good clients. I will never forget the manager of a car dealership— great income, but this loser ran Rich crazy and went and bought a new house without us. In his mind, he just got to us first because everyone takes advantage of everyone else. "Client for life" and "ethical transaction" were just parts of scripts to him. I'm never impressed with a client's income; I want to be impressed by the person. Don't get too carried away here; at the end of the day, everyone needs to qualify for a loan.

Some rocks pay

At the end of this chapter I tell the story of a couple who moved from Alaska. We let a few questions hang that we could have asked, and everyone paid for it. You will like this informative saga, but these were totally deserving salt-of-the-earth good guys. We were committed to making the deal work no matter what it took. Not everyone we meet is, though. A few years ago, we acquired a client, or maybe he acquired us, who wasn't a good guy. Gerry G: Rich will never forget him; I'm trying to. This was a client I wanted to show to the door as soon I heard the way he spoke to his wife. "Shut up, I'll handle this," is not the way a "keeper client" talks to his wife.

Rich felt that since he was not *anybody's* mother we should let it go and find the guy a house. Gerry already had his financing lined up and Rich called the lender and verified this—right in front of the client. Rich is so subtle.

Finding a house proved pretty easy; Rich wrote a contract that afternoon on a big, 3-year-old home in north-central San Antonio. Gerry G took out a stated-income loan because he did not claim income on his income tax return. New car, lots of cash for a down payment, and $18,000 in income on his 1040 for the previous year; this is not the profile of a solid citizen.

The contract to closing was all right. Gerry tried to talk to Rich like he talked to his wife and had to be straightened out, but only a couple of times. By this point I could tell Rich had stopped having fun, but he knew better than to try to get me to talk to the guy.

One of us always visits buyers after closing to make sure the house is okay and life is good. This is also a great time to drop off a gift and pick up a referral. Rich stuck with the system, but I doubt he was looking for referrals. "A" people refer other "A" people, and this guy's letter was much farther down the alphabet.

Rich was hot when he returned. This egotistical maniac had finished out the garage and had eight people on the phone doing telemarketing. It looked like a third-world sweatshop. He had put in a pool and poured concrete over the entire back yard, right up to the fence, after Rich had discussed real-estate setback lines in detail. By this point Rich had only reached disgust. It wasn't until he demanded that Rich help him with the home owners association complaints that Rich lost it. Gerry G claimed we had not told him about the existence of the association in this *gated community*. When Rich reminded Gerry of the disclosure he had signed when he made the offer to buy, the guy sent his wife out of the room and started talking about attorneys. Of course, Rich fished his van keys out and hit the door.

If we were panning for gold, Gerry G would have been a rock, at least as a person, but we got our commission. How could we know he was going to set up a business in a good community, blatantly breaking the neighborhood covenants? At least this far Rich was right to work with the guy. In fact I doubt that we would have gotten a good answer if we had asked about what he was going to use his home for. Somehow I can't picture my husband asking, "Now, ah, Gerry will you be setting up a third-world-quality sweatshop in the garage, or just parking the Beemer there?" The question would have been stupid and nothing would have changed. This guy was a loser as a human and the system couldn't change him or screen him out. He had credit and he wanted to work with us, but we don't have to put him on the mailing list.

Saving money is expensive

In the case of the Alaska people, we should have gotten more details up front; they were as candid as they could be. Even in retrospect, I doubt that we would have asked about the survey issue when they bought the previous home in rural Alaska. Not to steal the story's thunder, but the problem was a common one. The buyers were paying cash and the seller didn't see any reason to get a bunch of agents involved. Why spend money on a "simple deal" when the seller knew a good agent who would write it up for them cheap. I bet he did!

The problem was that cash deals don't require surveys, appraisals, or inspections because with no loan to approve, there are no underwriting requirements to meet. The folks "saved" $350 by using the eight-year-old survey the seller had from his original purchase. This worked fine until the person buying their house had it surveyed. Then they found out the previous owner had built a deck across an easement after he moved in; that, of course, was not on the survey. They knew the deck was not on the survey, but they did not understand the title issues involved with building in an easement area.

Now the new buyer's lender wanted it removed before approving the loan. Lenders always get excited about clear title issues; it's just their nature.

Of course statements like the seller "knew a good agent ..." stands my hair on end. Have you ever heard of a couple in a divorce sharing an attorney? But this happens all the time in real estate. People will write out a check for $150,000 or sign for a $200,000 loan and not have anybody on their team to consult with! It amazes me.

We worked through the problems, as you will see, but to do this we had to talk to everyone we could think of, not just the parties who should have been able to help. Problems get solved when you take action and tell people what you are doing. The world is really a small place. If you ask enough people you can solve your problem. If you don't get active and get some results during the day, you get to go home and worry about it all night.

Update systems beat Murphy

Next is a touchy issue. When working with out-of-town buyers, you will be thrown into contact with their other agent, the guy or gal selling their house back in Iowa. Typically this puts us in a dependent position. If the other guy drops the ball and the house in Iowa doesn't close and fund on time, I don't have a closing here either. Moving vans drive up to locked houses, people end up in motels rather than houses, and the whole thing can get to be a mess. *Usually* you can avoid this with a lot of communication.

As soon as you know the buyer's situation, call the out-of-town agent. Don't rely on your clients to keep you informed. They don't even know what features they want in a new house. How can they know what information you need to evaluate the probability of closing? That is not their job anyway. I believe that H.L. Mencken said something like, "Nobody's ever lost money underestimating the intelligence of the general public."

In the stories that follow, keep in mind that Murphy's Law (if it can mess up, it will) is basically a myth. Competence and systems will usually smooth the way for you, but when something bad happens don't sit on it. Go into action, communicate, and ask for help quickly, continually, and persistently.

Is My Buyer First in Line?

Recently we got the truck bug. We did not catch it from an urge to look cool or macho, but rather from the need to haul stuff around to rental houses and the desire to get a lower car payment. Vehicles are tools like hammers and computers, but more expensive. Well, I called a friend who used to be in the car business. He was my sales guy until he changed jobs and we got him to refer us to an honest, knowledgeable salesman. The sales guy he recommended was Tom Fadden, and "the old boy knows the business, Pam; you'll like him," I was assured.

We set an appointment and headed down to the lot. Wouldn't you know it, the right truck was in the lot and we passed it on the way in. This was going to be Tom's easiest deal ever. And, I hoped, his quickest, because sitting around a car dealership is not my idea of fun.

We gave him some information about ourselves, and told him what we wanted. Rich showed him the truck. After a few well-chosen questions about our needs and requirements, he did not go back to the desk to write it up. Old Tom went to the office to check the status of the truck in question. "I want to make sure you're first in line."

As luck would have it, someone else was already writing it up. This was no big deal. In fact, the one he found us was a better deal (by $1,985) and more the vehicle we needed. Tom knew his business and he was careful not to let us get involved any more than necessary with the first truck until he knew we could have it. He wouldn't unlock it until he checked.

In the car business, Tom did not have much trouble finding out if his client was first in line. In real estate it is often not as clear-cut, but it matters a lot more.

About two years ago we had a newly divorced client, an Army officer, whose name was also Tom. Fresh out of a dead-end marriage and coming to a new post (Army-speak for transferring to a new town and getting a new job), Tom was in good spirits. He wanted a basic house with a good commute to work and a living room large enough to pack a parachute in. His big passion in life was jumping out of perfectly good airplanes and seeing how close to the ground he could get before opening the chute. Of course when he explained all this it sounded better; in fact, parts of it sounded almost logical, until you think about it. Since I am his agent, not his mom, I asked how big a living room he needed and moved on. Years ago, Rich went though a brief phase of parachuting, but got over it. Personally, I have never felt the need to jump out of an airplane.

In this business, guys like Tom are gold. He had credit, knew what he wanted, and knew when he wanted it. All I had to do was find a house that delivered the goods. This we did in short order.

Sensing an easy transaction, I checked the house out carefully for any mechanical issues and we ran the numbers. Our offer was accepted after only moderate table-pounding. I knew the other agent and considered her competent if not real strong. She knew the technical niceties, but seemed to have to discuss all the little stuff with her client. I didn't sense the usual level of trust that exists between a seller and the person he selects to sell his home. Of course, some people are just not friendly.

Because of the option period, we always do inspections early, and this house turned out as clean as I expected it to be. Except for the nagging negative feeling I had about the personality of the seller, this deal was coming together nicely. Then I got the title commitment.

One of the major things that title companies do for us is check out the title on a subject property for mechanic's liens, tax liens, and any other unsavory items that could mean the seller can't sell it or that the title is "encumbered." The report is called the title commitment and it has four sections; look at them all, but really read Section C.

At this point in our story, it is important to understand the most basic phrase in our industry: real estate. The second word is easy—an estate is what you own; but the first word does not mean "real" as in "it exists." Real refers to the king as in royal, regale, *reale*. To be precise, the term refers to "the king's estate." We get to live on it only as long as the king lets us, because he ultimately owns it. Even though in the U.S. we are a little short on kings, the rule still holds. As long as we pay taxes on the property and don't owe the government any other money, we can pretend to own property. Tax is our rent. Once we stop paying it, we lose the lease, which here is called a deed.

In this case, Section C of the title commitment had the words every agent dreads: Internal Revenue Service. My client was not first in line for the house.

The seller knew he was in trouble with the IRS, but did not see any need to tell his real estate agent about an income-tax issue that went back to a nasty divorce two years prior. Just to keep it interesting, the guy was two months behind on his payments, plus he owed the Feds more money than he was getting out of the deal. To sell the house under the contract we had, he would have had to bring about $4,000 to the closing. He didn't have enough gas money to get to work, but he seemed determined to get to bankruptcy as fast as he could.

To this day, I do not know if the seller lied to his agent or if she was just intimidated by the guy and did not explain the part of the listing agreement that covers this omission. When the thing blew up on us, my client's options were limited. He had to have his household goods delivered; his storage time was almost over. Suing a guy with no money is generally a waste of time, and when you are third in line after the federal government and a major bank, it is also foolish. So we did what most not-to-be-pushed-around guys do, we cut bait and ran with the earnest money in hand.

This story has a happy ending. Again, as luck would have it, we found a better house at a lower price that had just gone on the market—two doors down on the same side of the street. Tom moved in after a relatively quick closing and just loved the house. The first house lingered on unoccupied until the bank took it back. The seller lost his house and his credit, but got to keep the IRS debt.

A big part of the reason the closing on the second house was only relatively quick was an unusual insurance issue. Dear colleague, let me digress and inform you.

As I mentioned, Tom was a solid citizen and Army officer, and the house he was buying was an average house in great shape. The issue of homeowner's insurance was just a formality to my mind. He had the insurance company's number and I told him when to call. What happened next was a lesson in why you should stick to business when you are doing business. Tom got to talking to the insurance processor, just chatting. When Tom talks, he brings up his life's passion, skydiving. It did not occur to me that this could be an issue or I would have warned him. When he mentioned "skydiving," the insurance company refused his application. Their reasoning was that if he was a skydiver he probably packed parachutes (good thinking so far), and if he packed the chutes in the house then they would be liable for damages if his chute failed. This was nuts!

By that standard, if he fixed a friend's car in his garage and the friend had an accident, then his homeowner's insurance company would be liable. I could not make any sense of this. By the way, we found out that insurance companies do not have to make sense *and* we don't get extra points for pointing out that they don't. Don't even think about their having a sense of humor. After a few calls, we dropped it and I recommended another company. This time Tom did not bring up anything. He answered every question honestly and shut up. This is probably a good practice for us all.

I have often thought about this deal. Ideally, when something goes wrong in a transaction we go over it until we figure out how to avoid it in the future. I have not gotten to that point with this one. If I run into it again, I will do just what I did the last time: stay on top of it, stay positive, and move the issues as quickly as possible. Flaky deals are not wine—they don't get better with age.

☙

You Can get Bit from the Strangest Places

Some years ago we got into business with a builder and agreed to market his small subdivision. Nice homes, good prices, and a marketable location. Eventually, we moved on because the builder, a smart guy, could not get the point that in the sales business, marketing is not an afterthought, it's the main point of the drill. Builders just have to build; that is what makes them tick. However, more normal people want to make sure a new product will sell before signing for the financing to build it. But before we declared him un-trainable, we sold a bunch of homes, one of them to the nicest family.

Generally speaking, nice, trusting people are more fun than the other kind. These were the fun kind. We met with them a few times, did a little redesign on a floor plan, and wrote up the deal. Their credit was great and they had a boat-load of money tied up in the house they were selling in Alaska. I called the agent there and checked out the situation and it seemed okay. It took a few calls to reach him, but Alaska is far away and it was winter. I honestly doubted I would have been in the office much during March in Alaska.

From what I could see on the internet, the Alaska house looked a bit over-priced, but what do I know about Alaska? I was not that concerned. Spring was approaching, the Alaska selling season was just starting, and we still had the house to build. I'm not much of a Sherlock Holmes, but I felt pretty good about this deal. I had checked everything out. The normal potholes were to be expected, but no big craters in the road as far as we could see.

Potholes have their own characteristics depending on the path you travel. If you have ever worked with a big builder, such as Kaufman and Broad, Centex, or D.R. Horton, you have found out that they don't change. Maybe they can't change. To get a non-standard light fixture is similar to turning an ocean liner. One takes five miles of sea room and the other 50 people to approve. Well, with little builders we have the opposite problem. I just love calls from the builder that begin, "Hey Rich, we got a good deal on this roof decking, so we...."

Reminding the builder about the spec sheet and the products that were promised to the client doesn't do much good. The next sentence is always, "No, you don't understand; they will love this stuff and it's half the price." Builders just want to build—agents and clients are only necessary nuisances. Thus, the lock-step building process of the big builders turns into a pretty open-ended operation for the small guys.

And homes get finished when they get finished. I've had so many conversations like this that I could write a book of "Unquotable Quotes." They generally start out, "Yeah Rich, I know nothing has happened on the house in two weeks, but we are waiting for the plumber. I know he is slow, but he gave the best bid for the work and he was only a little late on the last job."

A little late is like a little pregnant. Late is late when moving vans and apartment leases are involved. Of course, the agent is the one who ends up having to tell the buyers "we" have a delay.

So always make sure that the clients in a six-month lease can go month-to-month if they have to. They will have to.

Well, we knew about all of this stuff and I had made sure all the bases were covered; at least I thought I had. The clients had time to lower their price on the Alaska house, their temporary quarters had an extension clause, and the builder had good interim financing set up. I had even established good communications with the Alaska agent. We were determined that this easy deal would be just that, an easy deal. These buyers were very nice, completely trusting people—the kind you feel like you must protect. It was in this light that we checked everything out. Unfortunately, pride goes before a fall. Or closer to the point, I thought I was Holmes but was really Watson.

Let's fast-forward six months: the builder is now only a month-and-a-half behind. The house in Alaska is sold and getting ready to close. I'm looking at closing in 45 days and then it happened just like in the old movies, "The duke is dead; call Mr. Holmes."

The classic nice-guy problem occurred. When purchasing their house in Alaska our clients agreed to save the seller a few bucks and use an existing survey. This could have been all right except the seller had added a big deck that was not on the survey, but, "Who cares? It's only a deck." Nobody did care at that time. They were paying cash. They didn't need to "waste money" on appraisers, surveys, agents, title policies, and so on. Why people will sacrifice and save and use good judgment to pile up enough money to buy a home for cash, then get a case of penny wise, pound foolish at *the most dangerous time* is hard to figure out—until you think about it.

By the way, the most dangerous time is any time you are doing business in an area in which you are not an expert, or you are doing business with strangers, particularly strangers who will receive what you spend. Let me put this in perspective. agents commonly charge 5% to 7% to sell a house and split that with the buyer's agent. We usually tip 20% in a decent restaurant if the waiter doesn't spill wine in Pam's lap. Good help works for tips, so hire accountants, attorneys, and other professionals when you need them. You should remember this and tell your clients to do the same.

In this case, these nice people had done both things to qualify to be in their most dangerous time. They were not licensed real estate experts or any other kind of real estate experts, and they had just moved to this small town in Alaska and didn't know a soul. While they could have had 100 different disasters, the one that got them was the survey. The previous owner (the guy that sold it to my nice guys) had built a big deck across an easement at the back of the property that was not on the old survey. The new buyer's lender was not going to fund the loan unless someone got a variance or the deck was removed. (Remember, it was a *big* deck.) Most people don't pay cash, so they have to do all the steps. Of course, problems never come alone, or to put it more realistically, just one problem is usually not that big a deal. In this case the agent in Alaska proved to be just out to lunch. When the situation got complicated I could not find him and when I did, he was not much of an improvement over nothing. Our sale fell apart. I felt bitten. The nice people got worried. And the builder threw his hat on the ground, mumbling about interim interest payments.

Now I am not a big one for firing agents; they don't ask generals to sign deployment orders, it's the President who sends soldiers to war. Agents are too close to the battle, so we don't recommend firing other agents. But the clients were fed up, and this dog wouldn't hunt. We needed a new dog and we needed him now. What follows is important to know, dear colleague: don't just call a real estate office in a strange city and get the manager's recommendation for an agent or talk to the duty agent, unless the manager is your mother or you know the duty agent personally. You will more than likely get the new agent the manager is trying to help rather than the seasoned pro you need. In this case we required an experienced person who could price the house, handle the survey issue, and sort out a few legal matters. Short of going to Alaska and cleaning up this mess myself, I needed to find a contact I could trust.

After being in the business a while and going to national-level events, I have contact people in most states, as most of us do, I suppose. Alaska, however, is one of the few states that I just don't have a link to. More people live in Austin than Alaska, and I had never considered it a real market. Well, I had just met a lady who had moved from the city nearest to this property, which was plain dumb luck. I asked her who her agent was; she had rented, oh darn. Then I asked if she knew any one in the city still, and she mentioned a city councilman. Hot dog—they know everybody. Within the hour I had him on the phone and got the number of his good friend who "handles all my personal real estate." Within a second hour I had set her up with my clients. She turned out to be as competent as the councilman said she was. You can't beat a referral.

We closed on the Alaska house within a few weeks and then on the house down here, almost on time. The nice people did get taken care of. But I still felt bitten on an easy transaction.

Thinking about this deal after the fact, in my Watson mode, caused several things, or clues, to hit me. Of course, none of them would have escaped Mr. Holmes's keen powers of observation. First, the clients said they bought the house in Alaska for cash. The sloppiest deals are always the cash deals. This is because there are no underwriters to require a bunch of documentation establishing that both the buyer and the house are credible. It's elementary; there is no loan to underwrite. The second issue was more esoteric, but Mr. Holmes would have also deemed it elementary. The same habits of frugality that allowed the buyers to save the money instead of spending it on life's non-essentials set them up for the unscrupulous or uninformed seller and agent. It is amazingly easy to get people into trouble by recommending they do what comes naturally, which in this case was to save money. Not having an accurate, up-to-date survey and an appraisal done by a competent appraiser is not saving money; it is insanity. But to the frugal (and the cheap) the words "we don't need to waste money on…" are music to their ears. At any given moment any of us can confuse the siren song of self-destruction for a Willie Nelson statement of eternal truth.

൪

Dispossessed and Repossessed

The knowledge that we are susceptible to powers beyond our comprehension was old news long before Noah learned shipbuilding. But experience has shown that this is a lesson the Fates think is critical, since we keep getting reminded of it. Every now and again they reinforce this susceptibility with an inconvenient continuing education course in groveling at a time of the Fates' selection. We don't even have to sign up for these spirit-busting courses. Back in 2002, Lin Tin got an emotional master's degree in how doing the right thing doesn't always get you points. At first we thought he was a buyer client. Only later did we realize he was a cause.

Like Noah's story, this one begins with a big rain. Our hero is a middle-aged Vietnamese guy named Lin Tin. He is the person who would always win the prize for the one you would least likely notice in a crowd. You know the type, a classic low-profile immigrant. He had come to the U.S. when his country was wrecked in the mid-70s, and he came here largely because he didn't have any other options that sounded safe. After working for the U.S. Army for half a dozen years he didn't think the communists would set him up in one of the upscale suburbs of Ho Chi Min City, and "retraining brigades" had a negative ring to it. How he ended up in San Antonio I don't know. Communication was not fun. Lin couldn't speak more than basic English and we spoke even less Vietnamese. Just to keep his life interesting, he had lost most of his hearing in the war and had to use a lot of hand signs. But the guy was determined, and stayed on task until he got his point across. In fact he was determined about everything.

After a couple of decades of working, dreaming, and saving he got his family into a house and was on his way to living as much of the American dream as he could manage.

Then the rains came. San Antonio had 500-year floods in 1998 and 2001. This was an odd situation, given that they were so close together, but this fact is critical. The other critical point is that the politicians who run our city government have to be incompetent, since they can only run for two terms of two years each. So by the time they figure out what it is they are supposed to do, they have to move on. When the city council had to pay for flood damage in 2001 on the same houses that it had repaired in 1998, they realized they had a problem. Notwithstanding the argument that they may not face this problem again for another eight generations, they decided to be decisive. Lin's home and others on his block were condemned. He had to relocate his family and he had to do it in two months' time. The city had bought the houses and sold them to the developers that were relocating them. Lin Tin got $14,000 for his trouble and the down payment on the next house. Lin was dispossessed.

In a perfect world, Lin would not have had a real problem here. As you can imagine, he was one of those people who pays every bill before it is due. He should have been a mortgage lender's dream client. But remember this is life, not a romantic novel, and Lin was getting a lesson in susceptibility to uncontrollable forces.

Let's backtrack a bit. Just over a year before the 2001 flood, Lin's neighbor came over, and asked him to help her with some paperwork. The poor guy did not know enough English to fill out a loan application without an interpreter and could not understand anything without a deaf interpreter. Somehow the neighbor got his signature on her car loan as a co-signer. The best I could make of this was that the lady seemed like a nice person to him and she said he would not have to make the payments anyway. She just needed a co-signer so she could get the car. She really needed a car and he was a nice guy.

Now we don't know if they do co-signers in Vietnam or even if they have car loans. But here they mean something. The real reason a lender requires them is that he doesn't think the chances of the borrower actually paying the loan back are very good. In fact most lenders hit the co-signer as soon as the borrower misses a payment or two. In this case the nice person let the car "go back." Now our needy would-be homebuyer has been repossessed, and I need to know what is going on.

This is a great picture. I'm behind my desk, the interpreter is standing to the side (a nervous sort), and Lin Tin and his wife and kids are sitting with befuddled expressions in a semi-circle in front. I have no faith that the interpreter even knows what the terms I am using mean, and I'm positive he couldn't put them into Vietnamese sign language even if he did. We are going down a rabbit hole and I can't do anything about it.

In the end things did work out reasonably well. Lin got a house. But his loan was not at the interest rate that his frugality should have earned him. It takes years for your credit to recover from a repossession, even if you got the bad mark secondhand. However, for us the real issues here were broader than "don't co-sign." When Mr. Tin bought the first home it was not in a flood plain. His agent and appraiser had done their jobs correctly and checked the government flood maps against a valid survey. But the maps were changed after his purchase. When they want to, the Fates can move the goal posts after the kick is made.

༄

11 Listings, Mixed Blessings of the Real Estate Gods

Jeff gets a life

Some people just look like great sales people, and at major training events you expect to see this type of presenter. I was at a major event and what was curious about the next speaker was that he had sold $16 million dollars worth of real estate last year, with an average sales price of under $200,000. That is a lot of units and a guy that can do this must be a slick, focused dude. I wanted to see this guy.

Jeff looked like a professional wrestler as he lumbered casually to the podium to discuss "the listing process." He eyed the lectern as though it were some new device of uncertain utility and proceeded to stand beside it. When he finally spoke, I knew his day job had to be hitting guys with folding chairs in front of big crowds. The Brooklyn accent, huge muscles, and totally unassuming manner of a guy who had never been pushed around put him into a special category. I did not peg him as one of those rarified beings at the top of the real-estate food chain, a big-time lister. The blue jeans and sock-less loafers actually put him, at least in appearance, at the south end of the agent spectrum.

I'm taking the time to describe Jeff for two reasons. First, to make the point that you don't have to look smooth to list a home; an average guy appearance will do. Second, what he said hit the nail on the head. He knew what he had to do to be successful and did it day in day out without making unnecessary changes.

Sold while fishing

When Jeff started out in real estate he worked with a lot of buyers and was doing well. Feeding the family and saving a little, his first year was above average. One Monday he came to the office to follow up on the offer he had written the night before. It had been a successful weekend. The out-of-town buyer had been on time Saturday and by Sunday afternoon they had agreed on a house and signed the paperwork. Jeff was feeling successful. Six thousand dollars' worth of commissions lined up for two days work—not bad for a newbie. Then he noticed one of the guys in his office with two offers on his desk discussing the weekend's fishing trip.

This other guy had sold two houses while fishing; he had listed them. Someone else had had the fun of driving clients around all weekend while he fished with his kid.

"I ain't the sharpest knife in drawer, but I got the point."

Jeff changed his marketing as quickly as he could afford to do it, without dropping his buyer leads. As soon as it was practical, he dropped his buyer-oriented marketing all together.

When we heard Jeff give this pitch, his sales had grossed $16 million the previous year, and he had paid income taxes on over $200,000. More to his point, he had gotten his weekends back. Realizing he could change his business to suit his needs (or wants), he started getting some professional coaching. The first thing his coach did was introduce him to Michael Gerber's book, *The E Myth Revisited.* Jeff said he did not see any reason why he could not replace himself in his business. We could see his point: it takes a ton of listing appointments to get $16 million in sales and he was on track for over $20 million in the current year. He did not have many evenings free.

Almost two years went by before our paths crossed at a seminar in Austin. Jeff had made good on his reorganization. In fact, his business continued to grow at the same rate after he hired a listing specialist as it did when he was working four nights a week. Since that meeting he has gone on to finding a partner to help with management and hired a team of buyer agents to leverage the leads his listings produce. It seems that every time he replaces himself in his business, he develops a new, bigger, and more interesting business to work on.

4 It isn't Sold Until It's Sold

Or, How to Spend Money and Make It

Let's talk about what listings represent. First, they are leverage to the average agent. Leverage is not a mystical concept, it is simply getting more stuff done with the resources you have. The best way to think of it is as dollars per hour of work. My day has 24 hours in it and I make a good living. Bill Gate's day has 24 hours in it and he makes my annual income before his breakfast coffee. I use some leverage; he is massively leveraged. As an agent my problem is time. How can we get more productivity out of the day? This is a good question to ask every now and again, like every morning before coffee. I'm completely serious on this point: which activities make us the most money per hour worked?

Activities that pay

I have taken two listings in a day and I know agents who have taken three. In eight years, I have never shown houses to two different buyers and sold them both in a day. I have written offers for two buyers in a day but I had shown them houses before.

Here is listing leverage up front and personal. Once the house is listed, you have a 60% to 80% probability of getting paid. If you price reasonably well and showcase your houses, the probability jumps. Given that you can get an assistant to help with contract-to-closing issues and marketing, listing appointments are clearly more leveraged activities than showing houses.

Money accountability is the next big issue. Typically, listing appointments are developed from geographical farms and general public marketing. Both of these strategies are set processes. Let me explain and I will use farming as the example. If I am going to set up a geographical farm area, I am going to do a few no-brainer projects before ever spending a dime. Then I will do another set of activities for the rest of the time I am in real estate and want to have food with my meals. You see, farming in this business is not new and it has a few set procedures that every sane agent follows. If you get inventive, you will have problems with the "food with my meals" part.

Pick your paycheck farms

The first issue is to whom do I want to talk and do business with. Personally, all the owners of $500,000 and above homes I have dealt with tend to have either a god complex or more personal problems than I want to hear about. On the other hand, homes priced much below $150,000 don't generate enough commission revenue to compensate me for the effort and cost of marketing. By picking neighborhoods, I get to pick the size of my commission, since that is driven by sales price. If I like at least $5,000 paydays then I don't farm a neighborhood of $80,000 houses.

Not all communities are equal. In fact, none are. The point here is to pick an area that will pay off. To have enough turnover to be worth marketing to, your community must have at least seven sales per 100 houses. The magic number is 7%. One other issue: we never fight gorillas. If some other agent is listing 30% or more of the homes, we let him have it and move on to another area. There are too many areas that no one else owns for us to pour money into a losing cause.

The mind share game

Farming makes sense only if you are going to systematically apply a predictably successful marketing plan, one that gets mind share. Typically these plans are broken into three parts. The initial phase is to acquire mind share, a second phase of monthly mailings is to maintain mind share; and finally, giving an annual permanent item to residents to keep helps to sustain mind share between marketing events. When we start a new farming area, we begin with a phase one of mailing a set program of eight marketing pieces, one a week. This gets us known in the area and the residents begin to remember who we are, not just agents, but neighborhood specialists. After the eight-week program, the farm enters the sustaining phase. This requires a monthly mailing to maintain our position in the residents' awareness; it maintains mind share. This continues as long as the farm lasts. Finally, we send a "keeper" item annually. This can be as simple as a business card on a magnet for everyone's refrigerator to something as elaborate as you can afford. I don't think elaborate is better than simple here. I have listed a lot of homes with our business card on the fridge.

Leads starting at 11 cents

The point is that each of these items has a cost attached in time and money. If a postcard costs 50 cents to prepare and mail (stamp and materials), then a 12-touch program for one resident is $6 a year. A 500-house geographical farm is $3,000. The point is that if I spend $3,000 for the touch program and $450 on the keeper item, then the farm costs $3,450 per year for basic sustaining marketing.

I know this is getting boring, but a lot of people don't bother to do the math. So I'm going to finish.

If 500 homes have the target 7% turnover then 35 of them will hit the market. Now here is the deal. Farming dominance consists of listing 50% of homes put up for sale, and a successful farm is 30%. At the successful level, my share is 10 listings (35 X 30% = 10.5), and I target a 3% commission on a $200,000 average sales price. Or more to the point, my gross commission income, affectionately know as GCI, will be about $60,000. Marketing expenses for the farm, as we discussed above, were $3,450, or only 5.75% of GCI. This is known as a Great Deal.

Actually, this means that when you add up your marketing costs for the listings and the other name-recognition money pits, you can stay within the guidelines of spending only 10% to 12% of GCI for all marketing expenses. (See *The Millionaire Real Estate Agent*, pages 119 to 123.)

Just to re-run this: if the neighborhood only had a 2% turnover, and some do, instead of ten sales, you would only have three, if you were lucky. Is it worth the effort to do a farm for only three sales? On the other hand, if you choose a great neighborhood with high turnover and are successful, you can expand the farm as much as you want. An additional big plus for farming is that as the numbers in the farm go up usually the cost per item goes down. I spoke with Jeff two years after the first session I described above and he was doing twice-monthly touches to 25,000 homes at an average cost of $0.11 each. Unbelievable. He had a couple of high-school guys delivering his stuff every day after school.

Listing confidence equals practice

The other set process that Jeff had was his listing presentation.

Listing presentations are big deals if you want to sell a lot of houses. I want to explain just how we set the stage for success.

Confidence is the key to getting a listing and it comes from two factors that are totally under my control. This is important to grasp. For an average couple, selling a house is terrifying. They don't know what they are doing, often they don't even want to do it in the case of corporate relocations and the like, and they think they will look dumb or be taken advantage of. I can't honestly say they are wrong on any of these points.

Knowing that fear is in the air, I bring enough confidence into the house for everybody. My presentation is the means to do this. But before we get to the showmanship I have to discuss the prep. To say this is key is an understatement; it is much more important—it's critical.

Almost a decade ago, I went to an appointment and wasn't ready. I had great comparable sales, the history of the property, a beautiful comparable market analysis, and all the paperwork filled out except for the price. But I had been in a hurry. Normally I spent a few minutes laboring over all the sales in the area and looking for trends. If you feel like you know the area it comes through to the clients. Knowing that you are knowledgeable is like feeling the doctor is competent to the clients.

Not five minutes after we sat down, the husband asked about the house across the street that sold "a few months" before. *I did not have a clue.* When I researched this later I found out that it was 1,200 square feet bigger than their house and had a pool. What it sold for did not matter; it was not a comparable. But not knowing about it bruised my confidence and made the evening seem a lot longer. I got the listing, but not as comfortably as I would have liked.

The morale to this is to know your neighborhoods and don't miss the details. The other factor you are in charge of is practice. When you are sitting at the kitchen table in a $250,000 house with the possibility of making over $7,000 it is show time. Practice time is earlier.

To get a great presentation see your office manager or any one of a dozen good books. I have a few of the best in the appendix. Outline it, write it out, rehearse it into a tape recorder, and present it to co-workers, your spouse, broker, or anybody who is not supposed to pay you. The best practice is for me is the tape recorder. The number of times I repeated words, said "um," and added meaningless phrases such as "you know" and "like" was disappointing. I did not need a professional coach to tell me what to clean up. Remember actors and professional sports players are among the highest-paid people on the planet. They practice.

Don't practice here

I don't mean to beat a dead horse, but I can't tell you the number of agents who have said to me, "It will get better after you give it to a few more clients." As though they had client leads to burn. This is not how life works. Good hunters practice shooting at clay pigeons, and later hit the real birds. Great pianists practice at home and then perform in the concert hall. Instead of using clients as training aids, how about this approach: suppose that you played a recording of you giving your listing presentation in the car on your way to the listing appointment. Think of the state of mind this would give you, the confidence!

(Heck, it may also remind you what to say.)

One final issue needs to be put to bed before we get to the actual sequence of events at the listing show time. Technology is it. New agents and old ones who want to look up to date are always talking about PowerPoint presentations and getting on the internet at the client's house. I don't have much of an opinion of this. Personally, I want to get into relationship building and not a technical dog and pony show. But if you are comfortable doing it, knock yourself out. Just remember to make certain your show works every time. With your credibility and commission on the table you need to convey competence and not waste 15 minutes fooling with a laptop.

Showtime sequence

This is what the show sequence is and what it looks like. You may not want to do everything we do, but consider this overview.

The appointment is set for 6:30 PM. I have finished the research, gone over the listing presentation and my research, and driven the neighborhood for new listings and FSBOs. At 6:10, I call the prospect and tell her I will be 5 minutes late and ask, "Is this okay?" I wait for her to confirm it, and then ask if Jim, the husband, is home yet. I want to know that both parties will be present. Texas is a community property state; both members of a married couple must sign the listing paperwork. If one is missing, I cannot close for signatures. If he is not there or confirmed to be home very soon, I reschedule. The 5-minutes-late call is perfect to avoid arriving and having the husband say, "Just give me the presentation and I'll tell my wife." Talk about the worst of possible outcomes. I get to waste an evening, not get a listing, and get my information garbled by the husband as he compresses 25 minutes of well-thought-out information and consulting into a 3-minute monologue for his wife. No thanks.

Now back to our sequence. I arrive 5 minutes late to the minute. I park on the street in front of the house and get my electric measure, papers, and folder organized. I don't hurry.

Once out of the car I look at the house. You can tell a lot about a house and its owners by looking closely at it. I walk to one side of the yard and then the other, looking at condition issues, landscaping, and drainage, and driving the owners crazy. They knew when I was due and saw me pull up. Never look into the house when you pull up; you don't want the owners to see you looking at them as they peek through the blinds, and they will! I don't want contact yet; I want them to watch.

About half the time curiosity kills reserve, and Jim will come outside and invite me in. The wife usually makes the husband do the inviting; he is content to watch and knows I will be in when I'm ready.

Begin as the expert

This sequence sets me up as the house expert. Once at the front door I'm already in charge. I ask if it is okay for me to put my stuff on the kitchen table as I walk toward it. The next step is the walk through.

"Suppose, Mary and Jim, I was a prospective buyer; what would you like me to know about your lovely home?"

This gets the tour going and the clients talking most of the time. I am not particularly interested in what their opinions are about the features in an average house, but this is a great way to judge how these people will be to work with. The story in Chapter 6 about the 48 rocks, Leave It Before You List It, makes this point.

The other thing to consider is urgency of need. Remember we are all walking around inside the house and I'm asking about the children in the photos, any odd piece of art that seems like it is personal or of special interest to one of the clients. To the clients, we have not started business yet. They are often more open to discuss facts, such as when the new job starts in Dallas or how much they hate to move, or that they are just thinking about moving up and want to "do something" this year. Usually I have gotten a lot of this on the phone earlier, but I want to confirm it in front of both of them. It is amazing how the tone of things can change when both parties are present.

No rocket science yet, but I have accomplished a lot. At this point I am the house expert, I know the home's condition, I have confirmed the pricing against the condition, and I have confirmed the urgency of need. This is a lot. Next we go to the kitchen table and I explain the listing presentation. Then I write up the agreement.

The Truth in Storytelling regulations require that I interject a few disclaimers at this point. Every house is different and every owner is an individual. My goal is to always find some advantageous thing. It may be a feature or condition that will allow me to lock into my role as consultant. An example of what I mean may help.

Once a new agent asked me to go with her on a listing presentation. She felt she had bombed the first one. Now she wanted help and *needed* a listing. We arrived at the house near dark. I noticed some very heavy vines growing on the left side of the house during our little walk across the yard. As we did the "show a buyer tour," I stopped in the bedroom that shared the wall with the vines outside. The wall looked clean and I was surprised, but I moved a little night table anyway. Just above the baseboard was the termite trail under the paint. I touched this with my car key and a termite rolled out on the floor. Lost and confused, the little guy crawled under the baseboard while a yellow-headed friend peered out of the tunnel under the paint with antennae all a-twitter. The clients were mystified that I knew where to look and considered us real estate gods. With this credibility it was just a matter of writing them up and recommending a good termite treatment company.

In fact if you have enough credibility, you don't even have to get the listing to succeed. This happened when an acquaintance of ours, Erma, tried to buy a FSBO. The salty old dog selling this rundown dump was doing everything he could not to just get over on Erma, but be ugly about it, too. She asked me to go with her and help. I told her I could not represent her, but I could coach.

The seller's attorney had modified the Texas contract. I was glad I was present to explain what the provisions meant. She demanded that they be changed. Erma was so relieved knowing what she was agreeing to that in the next two years she sent us five great referrals.

In the next chapter, we will look at some of the messes commonly found on the listing room floor. Good pricing, professional marketing, and skill at negotiating and executing contracts goes a long way toward slowing down problems, but nothing stops all of them.

5 Know When to Fold

Or, Sometimes You Have to Leave To Get in

Positioning and standards are key elements of success. If you don't position yourself as the real estate expert and in charge of the sales and transaction processes then you cannot help your clients. Paychecks will get proportionately sparse.

Part of positioning has to do with the sequencing and knowledge issues discussed in Chapter 4, but those don't cover the entire issue. I have found that not all clients can be helped. Not all want a professional to help them, and some houses are just outside of what I am comfortable dealing with. The solution to this is simple. My practice generates enough leads that I don't have to work with clients who are marginal. Before we get into philosophy, let's discuss expertise.

I was not born knowing my standards regarding which properties I felt qualified to sell and what condition issues I could not deal with effectively; I had to learn a few things. We are not born knowing how to price homes, what condition issues buyers get upset about, or how long it should take to sell a house. However, we can find out these and a thousand other critical things by observation. It seemed apparent who the good agents were, the only ones worth watching. They got a lot of leads, listed a lot of homes, and made a pile of commissions, GCI. As my career has progressed, I found out that these traits don't actually cover it. Many agents don't price well and get a lot of listings; many spend all their GCI on advertisements for leads and have no take-home money. Remember in Chapter 4, I mentioned that only 12% of your GCI should go to marketing. If you spend 30% you will probably be busy, but may have trouble paying your mortgage.

Steal only the best

Once we decided who the good agents actually were, we previewed their listings. How were they priced? How good did they look; were they really "showcased"? To be blunt, we set out to copy the best practices we could find. When a good agent listed a home that sold in three days when the average number of days on market was 35, we wanted to see it. Very seldom does anyone care if you show a house during the option period. Later we asked a mega-agent for his showcasing checklist and that has been valuable.

I am belaboring this point because it is important. When you are standing in a house that is just not in condition to sell and you don't think the owners are going to fix it, or if the house is okay but the owners are not going to be reasonable and price it right, you have to be so sure of your standards that you can hit the door. In this first story we definitely had to rely on our values; if we hadn't, an aggravating situation would have developed into a real pain.

Icons and Armchairs

Some listings are a pleasure to work with. Some, however, are a different story. Different is the key word here. Our chiropractor referred us to another one of his clients, but this time with reservations. He knew we would do a great job, but he wanted to be sure we would not hold this one against him. These clients had a tendency to be difficult about everything, even chiropractic care. We assured him that we appreciated all referrals, not just the easy ones. Several of his referrals are now good friends of ours.

Rich called and made an appointment to see the house with every intention of listing it. The house had been on the market for eight months with another agent, but had no offers. This was strange to us because it was a newer home in a nice, gated community that had quite a lot of resales. On our drive into the community we did count six for-sale signs, and unfortunately this house was at the rear of the development. For it to sell, it had to be competitive. The sellers' current price compared well with the active listings. We drove up to the place wondering about condition and showcasing issues. What else could it be?

We were not even close to prepared for what was inside. The carpet was a rich, royal blue: very clean, very bright. The modest-sized living room was jam-packed with furniture, and none of it matched anything else. There was an avocado-green chair, a navy-blue couch, a burnt-orange chair and two huge end tables. The TV barely fit and no reasonable place to watch it existed closer than the kitchen table.

We asked the owners to show us around, "like we are buyers." Their tone had a hint of a whine that made us feel that we were wasting their time. In the entry, they had two framed pictures of Jesus, complete with real palm fronds, and three icons of the Holy Family in 18- by 11-inch gold-leaf frames. Another one of each icon was posted in the master, guest room, and kitchen, rounding out an amazing collection. The living room was full of statues and shrines. Two of the shrines had a figure of the Christ standing 15 inches tall in plastic, lit from the inside, complete with the Virgin and a saint kneeling before Him. It made *us* uncomfortable and we're not Jewish, Baptist, or Hindu.

The goal of staging a home is twofold. First, and very critically, I want the house to look well cared for (i.e., worth the money) and then I want buyers to be able to project themselves into the house. If they can't picture themselves in the house, they just can't buy it. It is that simple. If a seller had 40 pictures of grandchildren on the hall walls and 15 stuffed animals in the den and dining rooms, a young family may not be able to see past the stuff. It has to go. To leave the items on display hurts the seller because it slows or prevents the sale by limiting the number of prospective buyers who can feel comfortable in the house while viewing it. Religion is a bit different from either grandchildren pictures or Bambi's dad to some sellers; however, a distraction is a distraction.

It may be touchy, but staging was a real issue in selling this house. The average seller does not live in a chapel and the typical buyer doesn't want to buy one. These sellers conceded that the previous agent had tried to explain about staging as we walked through the house. We needed to know just how badly they wanted to move. Rich decided to fish for information. He asked what they had done about the agent's recommendation and they said they ignored him and he stopped bringing it up. We did get some good news on the walk-through. A new job was waiting in Washington, DC, and it was now time to go. And of course they blamed their agent for not selling the house.

We discussed pricing and condition. No issues. These people were, as I said, realistic on price and very good housekeepers. If you live in a shrine, I suppose you have to keep the floors clean. In any case the house was only three years old. Now it was time to walk on the thin part of the ice.

We got into staging. They did not like being asked to put the green and orange chairs in the garage and told us we were getting into their personal life. Then it got real touchy.

Have you ever told a new mother that her baby was ugly? I can't say I have either, but I believe the reaction would be similar to the one Rich got when he said, in his smooth, beating-around-the-bush manner, "And all the religious stuff has to get packed before I put a sign in the yard; and anyway, you have to pack them up for the move."

At first there was silence, then sputtering, followed immediately by words of incredulity. The wife asked Rich who he thought he was; did he believe in God, and so forth. He stated that religion was not the topic he was discussing today. But he said that we could sell the house quickly if they did what we suggested.

"How fast?" was their response.

The standard answer in our market is that a well-priced and beautifully showcased home should sell within 12 qualified showings.

They said they would list with us, but that the religious stuff would stay on the walls. We thanked them for their time and left politely and as quickly as we could get out the door.

This was all we could do. With six homes on the market in the same small community we knew the place would have to be competitive to sell. If the other agent had not gotten through to them in eight months and they gave us a flat "no" on staging, then why bother? The doctor is a great student of personalities and he had been right; they were difficult people.

A full two weeks later the wife called. She did not say, "How's it going?" or "Let's discuss the house." Her first words were, "We packed the items like you said."

True to her word, they had packed everything and moved the chairs into the garage. The house looked half again as large and would not be off-putting to a person of any faith or ethnicity. We listed it and started marketing it to agents who had sold homes in that area recently. (Note about staging: putting the big chairs in the garage did clutter up the garage, so it is not an optimal solution as a self-storage unit is, but staging the living room is more important than staging the garage).

About three weeks later after dogging Rich on every update call, the wife called us, very smug.

"You said we'd have an offer in the first twelve showings and we're at eleven; now what are you going to do?"

I told her we'd wait for the next showing and see how it went. Feedback hadn't been bad and we felt we were close.

Sure enough, the twelfth showing brought an offer. It was luck, but luck counts. We called the wife to tell her we thought an offer was coming in. This was a Tuesday, which we already had told them was our date night. We just don't, under almost any circumstances, work Tuesday evenings. She said, "If the offer comes in tonight, it's your date night; what are you going to do?"

I told her that if the offer came in tonight, we would see them with it in the morning and left it at that. Sure enough, we did get the offer. And, sure enough, we did present it to them Wednesday morning. The wife seemed particularly disappointed that she had not gotten our date night cancelled. She acted as if we had snubbed her, but we have standards about how we run our business. Who knows? Maybe she wanted a date night, too! The offer was clean; they took it. We left with the signed contract.

Despite having sold the home in only three weeks when it had been listed previously for over eight months, they could not be happy. We had made them so thoroughly angry about packing the religious stuff that they made it a point to tell the title company's closer that we were only average, and they were "barely satisfied" with our services. Guess our chiropractor was right—some people are just difficult.

The commission check went into our business account, but these people joined the bottom 5% whose names do not go into our database.

ଔ

6 Not Every Deal will Work

Or, DOA Happens in Real Estate, Too

Professionalism means something. As I showed in the icon story above, having standards and sticking to them is best for clients and agents both in the long run. The other side of the coin is that I believe I should help anyone who needs my help and who will work with me. We don't cherry-pick the good leads.

Another downside to being picky when you have a referral-based business is that you just about have to work with the people referred to you. Your referral source expects it. One past client referred his mother to us. She needed to sell a little $40,000 rent house. The place was a dump and older than dirt. But Jimmy is a good client and fine fellow even if he wears boots, drinks only bourbon, and has no taste for wine. We don't discriminate.

Rich got the place inspected and called our plumber, electrician, and handyman. I think the electrician made more on the house than we did. But it was sold in a week once we got it into shape. Jimmy's next referral was to a friend with a $600,000 house to sell. Cherry-picking would have been expensive. But even here we had our standards. The repairs had been all obvious and within our capability to manage. Not all repairs are.

If the time and effort are going to be too high we do draw the line, and you should too. Unmanageable problems have come in all sorts of packages. Some dysfunctional couples act like emotional vacuum cleaners. They suck up all your optimism into their vindictive machinery. They can be more destructive to your morale, quality of life, and career than a house ready to fall down with termites.

Often Rich and I go on listing appointments together not because we need to or even to make it a better presentation. It is just more fun. This next story was an appointment I missed, but I would have loved to have seen Rich's face when he grabbed the doorjamb. Of course it is a bit extreme, but still this story makes the point about having standards.

Termites

The call came in from an ad in a real estate book. These people wanted to sell their house in the worst way and did not know whom to ask. The house didn't meet any of our normal criteria. It was too small, out of our market area, and ugly, but Rich thought he would at least discuss it with the owners. The weather was cold and we had time.

Once in the house Rich knew they needed a lot of help, but he doubted much of it would come from him. He doesn't do demolition.

The part I wish I had been there to watch was when Rich tried to get out gracefully. I've hinted that tact is not one his strongest suits in life's great card game. Mr. Owner said, "Well, can you tell me if I have termites?" Rich, always testing Fate, asked, "Where do you think you have them?" The guy pointed out the jamb around the front door. The door was exactly where Rich wanted to go. Unfortunately he grabbed the jamb *over* the door.

The whole board came free from the wall into his hand. Where the board had been was the biggest termite infestation he had ever seen. I can't imagine his face, but it must have been a magic moment.

Rich said that he put the board back into place, and before it could fall off or the wall collapse, he ducked under it and escaped.

Just for the record, if you don't know how to find termites or know what the major conducive conditions are, attend a few home inspections. We have gone to hundreds and I learn something every time. The house in this story had wood siding extending down the walls to ground level. Our little white buddies could, and did in this case, travel from the dirt to the house without detection. This is a big deal because every termite must return to the dirt every day for moisture. Eating a house is thirsty work.

೫

Condition issues are actually the easy ones—at least we can see them and get an expert to explain them if we need help. The following three stories highlight the more complicated personality issues we have come across. Some ended well, as in the case of the seller who picked the wrong buyer. We had a lot of hassles and wasted a boatload of time, but we got a big commission and a lot of property management money to boot. The others did not end so positively. But life is a lot like that. In this business, and every business, a small percentage of deals are destined to bomb.

Finnegan's Saga

In the late 1930s, Europe was going down that historical slippery slope to war. Churchill said, "You can't trust the Fascists. They are not going to do what you want them to do." Typical of Sir Winston's statements, it sounded more profound than it was. His point was that dictators, like everyone else, do what they think is in their best interest. However, being dictators, they don't have to get permission from congresses or their wives before bombing things.

This is about the same situation the seller finds himself in when he agrees to that most nebulous of all possible ways to sell his house, the lease purchase. At this point I have made *my* point and we could stop here, with the statement: "Dear reader and colleague, don't ever get involved with one of these things." But the saga of Finnegan's sale is just too good to miss.

It started out like all great sagas with a routine event. You know what I mean: Beowulf was just paying a visit and Ulysses was just heading back to the house when their big adventures started. Bob Finnegan, an Air Force officer, had orders to transfer out of state and he needed to sell his home. We interviewed Bob and his wife, Kayla, at the house. It was a huge, 3,600-square-foot, three-year-old home, built by a good builder.

Bob wanted his questions answered. He was leaving in two

months for school en route to the new assignment, and too anal-retentive to leave any loose ends. He loved details. Kayla was much more particular. I thought I was going to be asked my blood type and mother's maiden name before we even got to pricing the home for sale. At the end of it, we agreed on price and marketing and listed the house for sale.

Everything was done in good order and everyone was smiling, but I just didn't feel the warm fuzzies the way I'm used to. They had looked as if they were thinking of more questions while we were answering their previous ones. Was anyone actually listening?

Any home with three small kids and a mother-in-law in residence will be a challenge to sell because of staging issues. But before Bob had to leave we got two offers at virtually the same time—one was great. It was $2,000 less than the other, but it was a regular conventional loan that would close in three weeks with a lease back. Kayla, kids, and grandmother could stay in the house until Bob found quarters at the new duty station. The buyers were not particular about the move-in date. The other offer was a lease purchase offer for full price.

My position was easy: "Bob, take the money and run."

Bob got involved in negotiations. The person making the lease purchase offer, Shana Watt, was a government employee whom Bob knew personally; they worked together. He didn't know her husband, Frank, the salesman.

Shana assured Bob that they could close in six months, no problem. She and her husband just had "a few bills to take care of" then they could qualify for the loan, according to their great loan officer. Her husband was—are you ready for this—a used-car salesman with a string of late payments as long as his arm. I am not saying all used-car sales guys have bad credit, just almost all of them that we've met. Once Frank got Bob's ear, the poor Air Force guy did not stand a chance. Frank could talk the bark off an oak tree, and he talked all the good sense out of Bob.

By the time I got an appointment the next night to go over

the numbers and convince Bob and Kayla to take the bird in the hand and not get lost in the bushes with Frank and Shana, they had been sold. Bob, always a detail freak, had worked out how he was going to get this great tax advantage by letting them rent for "a few months" for *less* than what Frank's house payment would be after they closed the deal. He had been convinced to subsidize Frank's rent. I lost it.

There are rules in real estate and Bob was breaking them like an M1 battle tank in a china factory. First, I told him that lease purchase agreements never go smoothly and usually don't work out at all. And second, you never, never, never write a rent-to-own deal where the money gets worse when you close. I told him he had to charge more for rent than their payment would be, not just more than his regular house payment.

"Bob, if you don't do this they will never close the deal and buy the house," was my last gasp. This deal was the best example of a negative incentive to close we'd ever seen and I was not communicating.

Bob patiently explained to me that I did not understand tax rules as well as he did and that he would net more money this way. He was right; I didn't care about the few bucks he would save on taxes. I was worried about a $170,000 deal and $1,500-a-month payment that could sink him and his family. I know how much Air Force majors who are not getting flight pay make.

I explained to Bob that I never do a deal based solely on a tax angle. Doing that is like picking a date for the prom based on the dress she will wear. In dating, it is the quality of the person or at least their good looks you focus on, and in real estate it is the deal. A deal must make sense as a deal first. (Once I did date a particular guy because I liked his family and he had a great car.)

The discussion got heated, because I am not doing my job if I let clients shoot themselves in the foot. Bob and Kayla were pointing a loaded 12-gauge at their feet. They got the idea that I just wanted my commission—now, and that they knew best. Plus, Frank and Shana were practically our friends, and "I would not lie to you." Meanwhile, I had checked out the Watts' agent and come to some conclusions. I didn't trust the buyers, their agent, or the agent's broker, and it would not have mattered if I had. The conventional deal was best for the sellers. They were moving to the other side of the country and needed the equity to buy their next house.

However, there comes a point when Pam the agent has to revert to basic principles, and we had reached that point. What they wanted to do was not illegal, immoral, or fattening. So I wrote up a short statement that said I advised against doing the lease-purchase agreement but that I would manage the property for my standard management fee of 10% of the rent until it closed. With no smiles, they signed.

Thus began the saga. The point about a saga is that it has a lot of unexpected events on the journey, and the hero must undergo a lot of challenges before he wins the Holy Grail, Golden Fleece, or whatever other trinket floats his boat.

The saga had started but I didn't realize it for four months. It was when I got on the phone with the Watts' lender to make sure we had everything set up to close in two months. The principals had agreed on a six-month lease. To my surprise, the loan officer said everything was great. Credit was good; pay stubs were up to date. I passed that on to Bob, now in New York. He made a "knowing" murmur and I thought about the taste of crow. Rich and I both had told him this would not work out and at present it sounded okay.

The week of our closing, Frank turned out to be three months late on his car. The lender had not actually re-checked credit before he had reassured me. I called Frank the salesman:

"How could you be late on a car; you've got a lot full of them!"

"Well, you know, sometimes things just happen," was the response. Clearly, we had a case of diverging levels of concern.

Coming apart was the next event. The Watts' lender decided that they were too much work and dropped them. Their agent quit the business. I stopped thinking about crow because I felt like I was holding the bag. We had agreed to manage the property until it closed and it still had Frank, Shana, and three kids in it. Occasionally, the rent was on time.

During the next 2.5 years, we were within days of closing four other times and never more than three months from a for-sure closing date with various lenders whom Shana dug out from under rocks. But it is plain hard to switch from a lease to a purchase when your payment will go up 200-plus bucks a month at closing. Both buyers changed jobs, both re-messed up their credit, and together they got Bob and Kayla very worried. This was why I had the Finnegans sign that statement about the lease-purchase being a bad idea. When a situation turns sour, human nature dictates that the guilty party find someone else to blame. In real estate, it is always the agent's fault. Bob and Kayla deserve full credit on this, they were as good as their word and never blamed us for the mess. However, the clock was ticking and the Feds were on the horizon.

In the world of taxes, there is a really sweet entitlement. In fact, it is the only completely sweet entitlement that common guys like us can use. It is the tax-free sale of your personal residence. The only requirement is for you to have lived in the house two of the last five years. A married couple gets to keep all the profits of the home sale tax free up to $500,000. Once you have lived in it for at least two years, you can rent it out for three years and still keep *all* the proceeds. A great deal by any standard.

The problem was that we were within a month of three years of leasing and the house still had not closed. For tax purposes, it had been an investment property for two years and 11 months. The Finnegans were on the cusp of a 20% tax bite.

I can't go into all the details of the loan issues and how we had to shift some stuff around. It got messy, so I directed the Watts to my lender of choice. Three days before our fifth for-sure closing date I just stopped calling. My assistant, Stevie, stayed with it, but we both knew that Frank had been sick. This was the second time he had been sick. The first time we got two unexpected late pays and his credit score had gone in the toilet again. This time the loan guy ran the numbers on just Shana alone and in the new job, she squeaked by on just her credit. The interest rate was not great, but better than I thought they would get. The loan would be in her name, but both of them would have to sign the title documents, since Texas is a community property state. The day before closing I got on the phone.

I explained to Frank that Finnegan did not care if his payment was going up $225 a month and I didn't care either. But I would make sure that Frank cared if this deal did not happen. In a calm voice I explained that if he did not go sign the documents at the title company, I had Finnegan's authorization to terminate the lease. I would personally get the sheriff to open the house and Rich would put everything the Watts owned in the street. The lease was over. Finnegan had realized he had nothing left to lose and finally let me do, as he put it, "whatever it takes, Pam."

You could say that this ended up a success. The commission on a $170,000 sale is not a bad payday, and for three years we collected $150 a month for management fees totaling $5,400. So in dollars I made three times my usual fee for selling a house. But the client lost and that kills the fun of it.

We all do as well as we can and behave as we think we should. Everyone has different standards. If you look closely, you will see that we don't even hide who we really are. A credit report reflects the actual person. If he does not respect commitments, he will not pay his obligations. Believe what you see. This is the client's book and they are telling you who they are. People do not change who they are or what they stand for.

ಜ

I was with Rich during this next story, but it is really his story and he tells it.

Leave Before You List It

It has been over five years since I got the referral to the Clay's house. It was a 25-year-old place about 20 miles north of the city. The tax records confirmed it to be in a nice area just into the Hill Country, not far from Canyon Lake. This place could have potential.

The Clays were not as young as they once were, Pete said. He looked to be a reasonably healthy 60-something. He didn't work but his wife had to drive downtown every day to her accounting job. She was tired of the commute. And it only took her two decades of doing it to feel that way.

Let me start at the beginning: a flaky friend referred these people to us and said they were really nice once you got to know them. It was that last part that I worried about, since I felt that way about her. When you list a house you have to communicate a lot with the sellers and they need to trust you and see you as their real estate consultant. I have found that it helps if I have confidence that the clients are wrapped well and mean more or less what they say.

This house needed either serious updating or a realistic price was my first thought, and the car had not stopped yet. The bad vibes started when the owner spoke. The tone conveyed the feeling that he was talking to "hired help." Usually people do this as a defense mechanism to hide a shortcoming of some sort. It did not make me comfortable, but this is business. How I feel is not really the point.

We looked at the place from top to bottom. I checked the pump, the pond, the baths, looked for signs of termites, etc. It had the oddest floor plan in three counties. It seemed you could not get to some rooms without going through others in sequence. The word cumbersome comes to mind.

Just as troubling were some of the eclectic features they had added to the house. The den floor was out of another century. The large stones set in concrete were so uneven I had to look down to walk across the floor. It reminded me of the floor of a castle, and the castle was not in good repair. The walls had very dark-stained wood paneling with an assortment of 14 dead animal heads on them. I could imagine unseemly things happening in this Gothic-novel setting and I wanted out of it. Equally clear was the fact that this room was his pride and joy. I was informed that, "Few people get to completely design a room in their house just the way they want it." Given this example, the practice should be illegal or require a license.

This descriptive stuff could go on forever, but we are discussing listing homes, not seeing kinky houses. What we did next was to try to get down to business. The kitchen was too messy to set my planner down. I didn't want to get something yucky on it. The den had a desk, but I didn't want to go back to that dark hole. So we all ended up in the living room. Just for the record, a living room is generally a bad choice for the presentation because it does not have a table to sit around and people tend to get too comfortable for work on the couch. As it turned out, comfort was not the problem.

The presentation went smoothly and we got to the pricing in short order. Here we hit the snag that I knew was coming. Now you can say with some truth that if a salesperson expects a bad outcome, he will get it. Likewise, much can be said for positive thinking. The problem is I went to graduate school in history, not acting school, so I just told him straight out what the place could sell for. If you have given me any part your attention, dear colleague, you have supposed correctly that his estimation of value was far north of mine. But you cannot imagine what happened next.

He rose from his chair with the dignity only the gravely insulted can muster and asked me to follow him outside. There, just outside the door that led to an irregularly shaped garden, was a collection of the ugliest rocks I had ever seen: all different sizes and various dull hues. They were completely unrelated in texture, type, or color to the garden. I could see no discernable sequence, but I made no comment, either. At this point I was keeping my own counsel. Pam looked at us expectantly from the couch as

Pete began to describe these rocks. One was from each of the 48 contiguous states and, "That one concreted into the sidewalk is in line with magnetic north." Somehow, sentimental value was supposed to convert to a higher sales price. All I knew was that the sidewalk was made hazardous with the lumpy gray rock partially embedded in it.

Pam and I got out of there as graciously as we could. I did not think that we needed a listing badly enough to take an overpriced ugly one owned by squirrelly people. I knew I did not want to work with a guy who had no tactile relationship with reality.

A few months later these people showed up in the newspaper. The accountant wife had been cooking the books of the company she worked for, and they were both arrested before they could retire out of state.

Some listings you're lucky to walk away from.

☙

This next story is actually a letter I wrote to the folks in our database a couple of years ago. It is about the difficulties of working with some people and in certain situations. Another issue that I want you to consider is that we sent this out to all of our past clients and friends. We have positioned ourselves in their minds as consultants and they expect this sort of frank and personal contact. This marketing technique is called a "letter from the heart" and is mailed monthly.

Fear of Being in Charge
Or, Why Don't We Get Help?

In this life we get to choose. Sounds pretty simple to me, but I am finding out it is not. In the past month, I have run into several people who did not know how this concept works, and it has cost them one way or the other. Of course, I discuss real estate stories, but the point goes much farther. Here is one of them.

A great young couple bought a "double-wide" because it seemed easy, and it was quick. They did not seek out an outside lender to ask about the financing issues involved in this type of purchase. As you would suspect, the on-site lender told them how easy it was. Well, it is easy getting into a loan; it is the getting out that's the problem. But they did not grasp the idea that they were in charge and could ask anybody they wanted to. The effect of this was that they only talked to people who worked for the manufactured-home sales company. If you go a Centex homes sales office, the guy working there will tell you that you need to buy Centex. Nothing wrong with that; Centex is paying him. This is the way the world works, in my opinion.

Why did these smart people fail to get the rest of the story? To me, it seems they did not want to check with an outside lender or agent because they did not want to bring someone else into the transaction that they may not want to use. We can be sure that the on-site lender made them a great offer on the financing and they felt that another lender might have offered some advice but would not be needed in the deal. It would be embarrassing to ask for information and then not use the other guy.

Well, here is what being in charge is all about. You not only can pick, but it is your responsibility to pick. Any ethical accountant, attorney, agent, lender, etc., knows and appreciates the fact that the clients will do what they determine to be in their best interests. This is the way the game is played. I have had to tell clients that I could not do more for them than the deal they had. I've also recommended that they leave the lender they had because the new home builder had a great deal and they would come out ahead by switching. This does not hurt my relationship with my favorite lender. He knows that people should do what is truly in their best interest and that I will send him more business.

What all professionals hate is seeing good people not get the information they need and therefore making poor decisions. These poor decisions are usually made because the client, the average citizen, just did not feel confident enough to keep looking for help until he or she found it.

The next time you are in front of a difficult decision, take responsibility for yourself and get the help you need to make the best decision for yourself. Don't let anyone make you feel pressured or in a hurry. If it is a good deal today, it will be a good decision tomorrow, and tomorrow you will have the information you need to decide.

—Pam O'Bryant, Your Realtor® for Life

7 How to Build a Winning Team

Or, Get Your Clients to the Top of the Appraiser's Inbox

I always mention to every class of new agents that they are not in business until they have a client. This means that everyone's first job is lead generation. This rule works for every person and organization on some level. A dentist is not a dentist until he generates a lead (client) to sit in the big chair. All the support staff and vendors of the real estate industry work this way. A single client goes through a lot of hands.

The way I see it, no agent ever sold a house alone. We need a huge support staff of inspectors, lenders, title companies, repairmen, insurance brokers, and so on forever. From this group, you build your selling team. That team comprises a specialist in each of the areas I mentioned who knows you and wants to do business with you. We have an inspector, an appraiser, a lender, an insurance agent, and an escrow officer that we regularly use. We know how each other's business works and respect each other's time. These people need us to send them our clients, and in order to keep those clients coming, they provide superior service.

The rule here is that you have to give to get.

We have one home inspector whom our clients use. I know that many brokers require agents to give buyers a list of inspectors to select from. This is dumb. I am the fiduciary for my client and I know who is a good inspector and who isn't—do my clients? The last thing I want is my client unknowingly buying a house in bad condition or not buying one in good condition because a bozo inspector could not explain a problem correctly. Unless the client knows an inspector, I set the appointment and select the inspector. This also gets the inspections done when they are convenient for me.

Liability is not a real issue

What about liability? Liability is a condition of our business, but it doesn't work the way most people think. If a client has a problem and hires an attorney, the agent gets sued. It is that simple. I know of three inspectors in town who have errors and omissions insurance, E&O. Just three out of 54. If my clients sue an inspector, what can they get? He has no money in his business; his house and pickup truck are protected by the homestead law. All that's left is the briefcase, and most of my clients already have one. It is not an issue of the client's thinking, or not thinking, the agent did anything wrong. Somebody with cash or insurance has got to be named in the suit if the attorney is to be paid. That somebody is the agent. This is the real situation and I have figured out how to sidestep it.

We asked a lot of questions of the first eight or ten inspectors that we worked with. The errors and omissions insurance came up because even as new agents we had it and found out that almost none of the inspectors did. When we found a good inspector who had E&O insurance, we asked how it worked. He named us on his policy as a covered party and we sent our business to him. Simple deal.

This is the sort of thing we have done with our entire support team. By being loyal and finding out how they work, we have gotten a lot of loyalty in return. Here is an example of what I mean.

Manage risk

Three years ago, during the height of the mold scare, everybody was concerned about mold claims, especially insurance companies. Homes that had previous water-damage claims, roof repairs, and almost any plumbing claims had their insurance rates hiked through the roof. Because of existing policies, often the current owner was not immediately affected. But the new owner, my buyer, would be hit. This was a big deal.

One house we put under contract was assessed at three times the normal rate and the deal died. Unfortunately, this disaster did not surface until after the buyer had bought an inspection (which was clean), an appraisal, and a survey. My client had $1,000 down the drain, but he couldn't buy a house with homeowners insurance at $2,900 a year instead of $850, about the normal rate. This was not an overt "failure to disclose," because the current owner had no idea that getting his roof replaced would multiply his insurance costs. The house was in great shape and the owner was proud of it. Now, Larry, our insurance guy, checks any address we give him for problems. He doesn't get to insure all of these houses, but he has a chance at all of them. More importantly my clients don't have bad news a week before closing. This is not avoiding problems, rather, it is fear management.

Sometimes clients just like a house and will buy it even if it is in a flood plain or has high insurance premiums. That is not part of my job. I'm responsible for getting them the information. Clients get to decide how to spend their money. Remember, my main job is managing their fear, and one way to do this to provide information and options.

Expertise is another issue. I don't know the ins and outs of inspecting, insurance, or appraisals, but in the course of business I have questions that need answers. Imagine this scenario....

A Hot Day and a Cool Deal

A family whose house we had just listed a few streets over had referred the Stiversons, our new clients, to us. The house was beautiful and at an $80,000 higher price point than the house of the client who referred them. Jim Stiverson was leaving in a week to start his new job in DC, and Lynn was staying with the teenagers until school let out in about 45 days. They really wanted the house sold before she left.

The only condition issue was the over-spray on the rock veneer. This was a beautiful rock house and Jim had saved a few bucks by hiring the lowest bidder to get the eaves stained. Now he had an ugly spray line 12 to 14 inches wide all around his rock house. It looked terrible and he did not know how to handle it. I called my painter and he said "no problem." Of course, that is what he always says. The issue was the rocks were aged; the house was 17 years old. I did not want a clean strip around it any more than the over-spray. The aged-rock look is a selling feature in the Hill Country.

It turns out that if you spray a one-third-strength mixture of a certain solvent and water on the over-spray, then lightly power wash it in *40 seconds,* the paint comes off and the aged look stays. It looked impressive and Jim thought it was cheap at $500 to make his mistake go away. We all have egos.

The house sold in five weeks, which was quick for that rural area. Our buyer was pre-approved for his loan and wanted to close in three weeks, which was in line with Lynn and the kids' desired departure date. The only problem was that the lender needed the appraisal within a week if he was to get the loan done. This was during the peak real-estate sales month in San Antonio and everyone was busy with long backlogs. Our appraiser's secretary told my assistant he couldn't get to the house for nine days. Rich made a call and explained the situation and had the appraisal done and delivered in three days. We don't call often, and only call when necessary. People appreciate that.

Rich met the appraiser at the property on an afternoon that hit 96 degrees with 90% humidity. He made sure everything was unlocked and offered his help. Partly, Rich just wanted to be helpful because we were getting a favor done, but he was also making sure the appraiser had the comparables he needed. We wanted to make certain that the house would come in at or over sales price. If there had been a question, *any question at all,* about price, Rich had our comparables in the van. They weren't needed in this case, and Rich didn't mention them. Appraisers are picky people by nature. The last thing you want to do is come across in a way that looks like you are questioning their expertise. We always use the consulting approach when discussing price comparisons and we always say thank you for favors.

I would never send an appraiser a present for getting the right value on a home. That would smell off-color. But to move my client to the top of the in-box, which allowed us to close a big transaction, deserves more than a Hallmark card.

Rich dropped off a bottle of single-barrel bourbon.

ଔ

The Golden Rule of Reciprocity

This story would not have had a happy ending if we had not already had a couple of relationships. The appraiser knew Rich really needed help; he also knew we had sent all the business to him that we could that year.

Bluntly stated, we went into the marketplace and found good people to help our clients. We know what their strengths are as well as their weaknesses. Our plumber tends to be messy, but cheap and on time. Our A/C guy will repair it if he can and not just keep putting in new parts until the thing works. We know these people and we are loyal. This has gotten us good service in our home and investment properties (more on that later), and helped us take care of clients. We never want our clients to feel they have to go to the Yellow Pages to find an electrician. I want my guy to get the business and I want a chance to be helpful to past clients. Never forget the Golden Rule of Reciprocity: *If I help you, I get to ask for a favor. And I always need qualified referrals.*

Reciprocity can help your business and build your relationships, but you have to use it correctly. Here is a tip: all of our current and past clients know that we have a vendor or craftsperson for most problems around the house. They call all the time for plumbing, electrical, A/C referrals. I refer the right person to them professionally. I don't let them call the electrician, I call him and then have him call the clients. This puts me in charge of the referral and ensures that my craftsman gets the business. A couple of days later, after the repair, I call the clients to ask if everything is working. Usually they say, "It's great Pam, we loved him!" As long as the response is positive I use that moment to ask for a favor, and it is the favor I always need.

"I'm glad I could help. Because of the referrals we get from our clients we have time to line up these vendors and craftspeople. Who is the next person you know at work (at church, school, etc.) who needs our help?"

Even if this doesn't get a lead on the spot, it keeps the referral idea in their minds. You should also notice that I used this as an opportunity to model the correct way to give a referral to my past clients.

Staying in touch is the other key point. But I don't just mean keeping everyone updated on what is happening. An update call, in my opinion, is the best tool for keeping me informed. Once a week I call the agent representing the other side of the transaction. Buyer or seller agent, it doesn't matter. I keep the call short and to the point. After a greeting I give the agent any information I want her to have. They always thank me for the information. That "thank you" is my permission to ask a few questions myself. If I'm representing the seller, I will call the buyer's lender once a week and say hi. Now, this person does not need to give me the time of day, much less an update on his client, a person I don't represent. However, remember what I said about leads. A dentist is not a dentist unless someone is in the big chair. Well, a lender is only a rate watcher if he doesn't have a borrower in front of him. This guy would like to do business with me. He wants my referrals. If I allow him, he will try to be helpful as possible.

I call once a week and offer that opportunity.

I know a lot of agents who ask their clients about transactions and not the other professionals involved. I suppose we are shy. But as I have mentioned before, if a client is from out of state you can't expect them to know the pertinent details of the New Jersey sale. If that deal does not happen, and happen on time, I am holding the bag here in Texas. This is a point to ponder.

Remember, my clients did not comprehend what they really wanted in a house until we did a needs analysis and they saw a few. How in the world can I expect them to know what is important in the technical process of selling and closing a deal? I need to ask the pros. I want to know that the buyer for my client's house has an approved loan, and has insurance on the house lined up. I need to know if there are lender-required repairs and that the place has appraised for the contract price. The list goes on and on, but you get the point. Of course, not all agents are easy to work with and sometimes they are just not helpful at all.

If the agent in New Jersey is not forthcoming on my questions, I mention it to my clients forcefully. The guy is supposed to be working for them just as I am. If he is dropping the ball, I don't want my clients to be surprised.

When to worry

Avoiding surprises and diagnosing problems early is key. Deciding what information is necessary and then getting it is one way to do this. Let me give you an example. We listed this house for $110,000 near an Air Force base. An agent from a little two-man real estate company showed it, and the buyer made an offer based on 100% VA financing. We have sold dozens of these. But I am always concerned when a buyer has not committed anything to the deal. Without commitment (and commitment is money in this case), it is very easy for the buyer to walk away from the deal and my seller will have lost irreplaceable time on market.

We look for several key signals of commitment. If the buyer does not get the house inspected during the option period, the deal always dies. If the buyer has the place inspected and tells the inspector to bill him at closing, the guy is thinking about walking. If the buyers don't provide the documentation the lender needs to process their loan or the buyer delays on lining up homeowner's insurance, we know we have a problem.

Of course keeping people updated is a two-way street. I want the agent on the other side of my transaction to know that we have things in hand and to be able to reassure her clients that all is well. "The less panic in a transaction the better," are words we can all live by. In this next story we ended up buying an investment property, but notice how we keep the underwriter informed and used our vendors to good advantage.

Watch Your Step

Our buyers were looking for their dream house in a nice little community in the north-central area. They could go as high as $80,000 without a nosebleed, but even there they were almost out of air. They really wanted the location and good schools. So we were looking at the bottom of the barrel for the area. The good stuff started at about $95,000.

After viewing a couple of foundation problems and nasty messes, Rich drove them to the house on Queensway. From the outside the place was great: a two-car garage, corner lot, and the roof looked good. The privacy fence was not impressive, and the tall bushes and bamboo looked like someone had hired Tarzan as the gardener, but all this could be fixed.

Inside, it had the look of a suicide bomber's work address. The carpet was torn and dirty in the places where it wasn't gone altogether. To say it looked rundown did not begin to describe the place. But the real winner in this nice four-bedroom was the dark wood paneling in the family room. Not that paneling is always bad, but this stuff was loose from the wall. The yellow sticky notes all over the wall saying "termite damage" should have given it away, but Rich pulled on the paneling anyway. (I suppose it is just who he is.) The termites were like sharks at a dead whale, in a complete feeding frenzy.

The buyers wanted to leave.

Rich quickly explained that at this price, $78,000, the place was a great buy and some "sweat equity" would dramatically increase the value. Fixed up it was worth over $100,000 if it was worth a nickel. But the vision of thousands of termites was all they could see.

They got in the van.

At this point in our lives, Rich and I had decided to build an empty-nester home for ourselves a little outside of town but still only a 7-mile commute to the office. Our problem was we were out of time. We had sold (and closed on) our home. The nice buyers had been patient with us, but they wanted to move in to what was their first home. (Classic picky buyers) They kept saying things like "we want Christmas in our new house."

Our builder, like every custom builder on the planet, was behind in constructing ours. It was supposed to be finished at the end of November. Based on this we had talked the buyers out of having their Thanksgiving in the new home. But it was now October and we knew a November closing on our new house was *not* going to happen. A move was in our future, but *not* to our new house. We were as aggravated as we were disappointed and the options did not look good. Renting an apartment didn't even sound good. It was time to review all the options. Could we buy the termite-infested dog Rich had recommended to our clients?

We decided to do what every highly skilled and knowledgeable person should do, we asked an expert. In this case it was our underwriter, a civilized lady who worked with a big national lender. I explained that we had sold our house and were in the middle of building another. Our construction loan and permanent financing for the new house were already in place. Of course she knew this. Would she let us have a loan to buy an investment property to move into until the new one was finished? Could we do this without killing the financing on the new house? We knew we could rent it out after the new one was ready. I showed her comparable rentals that demonstrated it would have very positive cash flow.

Only in America

Rich had run the numbers. His estimate was about $11,000 for fees and fix-up (the actual number came closer to $13,000) and we could rent it for $1,000 a month and be under the average rental price for the area. Our payment would be around $780 a month, $220 to the good!

The answer we got surprised us.

The underwriter said, "You can use owner-occupied financing if you intend to live in the home. If you decide to sell it after one day, that's your decision. In America, I'm not going to make you rent a home just because your new one isn't ready yet."

Philosophically, I agreed with her but we had never thought we would be able to get an owner-occupied interest rate when we already had a home loan approved. Not being one to check the teeth of a gift horse, I shut up and took out the loan. Rich scheduled inspections quickly. We had a house to fix up.

Matt, our friend and inspector, had a blast. He and Rich tore off paneling, switched on switches, and walked around in the attic. Matt said, "watch your step" several times. Later, Rich said he felt that buying this place *was* watching his step. Matt was concerned about a more immediate outcome: Rich stepped off the decking in the attic storage area and nearly landed in the garage below. This was a new experience for Rich and he says everyone should do it once, just for the thrill. Then again, he has jumped out of an airplane for that reason—maybe he meant it.

The inspection confirmed that termites had eaten a few studs and the plate over the den window, but the house was sound and the air conditioning/heat actually worked.

We had a chance to watch our vendors up close and personal as they put tile down, removed studs, did drywall, and painted. It adds a lot of credibility to be able to tell a client that the person you refer is "the guy that we use." But this was not the high point.

The real thrill is that even though I got a little crazy on fix-up, the cash flow has been great. The first year we got a gross cash flow of over 15% on cash invested (cash on cash return); now three years later it is just over 21% per year on our initial investment. At this level of return, we can set aside substantial reserves and still pay this house off in 14 years. When paid off, this investment property will be contributing over $1,000 a month of our mailbox money. It will also be worth well over $150,000 at that point if we should ever need the cash.

Just for the record, we did not get to move into our new home until March, since the builder ran four months late on completion. But the lesson we learned about financing and the positive experience of fixing up Queensway made it worth the trouble.

Rich may have gone into the garage a bit casually, but if you watch your step in real estate you can do okay.

଴

III The Closing Celebration

Or, Knowing How to Get Paid and Paid and Paid

Closing is the term we use to conclude a contract. We close out a contract when the deed of trust is signed. It's a celebration because the sellers just got rid of the house they did not want to own, the buyers got one they wanted, and I got paid.

If you think this is the point of it all, you missed the boat.

8 Moving to the Next Phase

Or, Setting Up Future Paydays

One of our longtime coaches, Joe Stumpf, runs a nationwide coaching organization, By Referral Only, Inc. Annually he confers with agents, lenders, and investment planners in almost every state. He looks at how the best practitioners do the business and what systems work the best. One of his biggest "ah hahs" concerned referral percentages. If a client refers someone before closing, during the time between first contact and closing, that client has an 80% likelihood of referring someone else within a year after closing. Think about that one.

We have found this to be true. More importantly, this is the easiest time to get referrals. During this period, we are in touch with clients almost every day, at least weekly. At no other time will this be the case. It is the time for us to get mind share with our clients and it is the time they can see referrals best.

When everyone is pregnant

Think about how the brain works. Once we bought a new blue Volvo. It was the first year of a new model. We thought we were unique; we couldn't remember seeing another car like this one. On the way home we saw someone else driving "our" car. Of course, that model had been on the streets before, but until we were familiar with it (and when you pay for something you are familiar with it), we couldn't see it. As soon as a woman finds out she is pregnant, everyone she meets is pregnant, or at least it seems that way.

Buyers work the same way. Once in the market, they see for-sale signs they never saw before. They hear conversations they never paid attention to before. What we want our client to do is interject us into those conversations. This is not as simple as it would seem. NOBODY knows *how* to refer. It is like tying shoes; you have to be taught.

Dialoging for dollars

Here is a typical situation. We have met and exceeded the client's expectations in a transaction. This is nothing special. We are supposed to do a good job for our clients. However, during this process "referable" moments occur and we take advantage of them. Suppose the appraisal comes in low and we represent the seller. I will pull out our comparables and put the information forward to the appraiser to justify the sales price. This is information we have on hand from pricing the house in the first place.

Rich will then call our client with a set dialog. He states the problem, "Jim, remember we told you selling a house was like an airplane ride, it could have some turbulence."

Jim, the seller, will give a hesitant, "Yes."

"Well today we ran into a bit of a storm." (Rich makes the problem sound significant.)

"The house did not appraise at sales price. This means the buyer would have to come up with more out of pocket money to buy your house or we would have to lower the price to keep the deal together."

Jim doesn't respond, but Rich will hear him gasping for air at the other end of the line.

"Pam jumped right on the problem. She found some comparables that met underwriting standards better than the ones the appraiser was using and he accepted them."

Jim: "What does that mean?"

"It means we got the value up and this problem is behind us, so we'll still close on time."

Jim will respond with a "wow," or "thank goodness," or whatever and follow with a "thank you!"

During the next 15 seconds Rich has a referral moment to deal with. The dialog for this is, "Thanks for noticing. You know, the reason Pam has the time to stay on top of your transaction so closely is that because we get so many wonderful referrals from our clients, she doesn't have to spend all her spare time looking for business. Who is the next person you know that needs our services? We are looking for great people just like you."

Then silence. Rich lets the client say the next word even if he has to wait two minutes. If the client talks first, he will at least be trying to think of a referral. If you do this process well, you will get referrals.

When the client gives Rich a referral, Rich does a little training. Remember, nobody knows *how* to refer people. Rich will ask for the whole name, phone number, how the client knows the referral person, how well he knows her, and why she wants to buy, sell, or invest. Then he asks when is the best time to call. With this much information Rich is ready to make a good call to our *next* client.

Current client gold standard

Imagine you will get to use the referral script several times during the transaction by just adjusting the words a bit. The gold standard is to get 50% of our current clients to find us our next client. The effect of this on our business is wonderful. We gauge how well we are meeting our client's expectations by the percentage of them who give us referrals. Our main measurement tool is also a major moneymaker in two ways.

By doing the teaching with our current clients, we are showing them how to give us referrals. Giving a stack of business cards to a client to hand out is a great waste of time and cards. We give the client one card and teach them to call us when they run into anyone who needs us. We want to be the ones to make the call; if we don't, it will never be made. How many times has someone given you a card and you just lost it? The truthful answer is almost all the time (except when you threw it away).

We did not appreciate the referral process at first, but using it consistently has built our business. By the third year in real estate we were at 50% referrals and 28 closings. This was not fabulous, but it was a good living. Even at low San Antonio home prices, our GCI averaged between $7,000 and $8,000 per month and closings were very steady. I only wish we had not wasted months before hiring our coach. It was difficult to re-educate the first year-and-a-half's worth of clients, and not particularly successful!

The learning curve caught up with Rich our first year in business and it put our refer-ability to the test with his first listing. This is a funny story now, but at the time it was cataclysmic. This was Rich's first listing and he tells the story. It may seem that he starts it off at an odd place, but the point is worth making.

Do It Right, You Make More Money

In the country everyone worked. Like most of my friends, I don't remember learning to milk a cow, feed hogs, or hoe corn. It was just too far back. But when I was 12, I reached one of the milestones of life: I got my first real job. "Real" meant two things in the country. First, it was not for family, so I could brag about it to the guys; and second, it was for money. I worked for a grumpy old farmer, Mr. Crossford, who had a big place behind my grandfather's farm. The job was seasonal; what job on a farm isn't? The drill for this particular job was to place a 15- to 20-inch length of sweet potato runner on the freshly plowed, sandy row. Then, push the middle of the runner down into the sand about five inches or so with a flat stick. Once the runner is in the ground, one tap on the dirt next to it would backfill the sand around the runner. This method plants the thing and it takes root.

If Mr. Crossford got more rain than insects, he made sweet potatoes for the local market. For those readers fortunate enough not to know the business end of a sweet potato, let me explain this curious plant. It looks like a handsome wild vine that covers the sandy ground in great green circles that interlock with other sweet potato vines and they will go up fences and over weeds. In the fall the leaves turn yellow and the potatoes are ready for harvesting, which is another seasonal employment opportunity.

Being a kid, it wasn't long before I got sloppy in setting the dirt back up to the runner after putting it in the ground, and old Mr. Crossford pulled me up short about it. He said that each one of these runners could make 25 cents' worth of potatoes. This was in 1958 and that was a fair amount of money. I was being paid a whopping 50 cents an hour.

He said, "Don't get in a hurry; do it right. You make more money that way."

I understood that to mean that *he* would make more money, but that was fair—he owned the farm. This old guy watched his business closely and I knew that very little happened on his farm that he didn't know about.

Later in the spring, my cousin Lee came down from Pennsylvania and we had the classic boyhood summer. We would get up at first light to shoot rabbits or whatever. At 12 you will shoot anything, and Mr. Crossford did not really care if we took a few cottontails out of his fields. Although we didn't know just how far "really" went, we knew we did not want to discuss the matter with him, so we were careful. He did not plow closely in the corners of his fields. In these areas mesquite trees, small bushes, and weeds provided cover for rabbits, quail, and other creatures to breed and live. Today we would call this an ecologically sound practice, but actually, the man just liked critters. Then the dynamic changed for us.

The watermelons started to ripen.

At 6:00 or 7:00 in the morning after a bit of hunting, *nothing* is as good as watermelon fresh-stolen from the field, still cool from the night air. The first week they were ripe we only took three and were very careful to carry them a ways from his field before busting them open.

At church that Sunday, I avoided catching Mr. Crossford's eye. This was easy to do because the Crossfords sat behind us on the other side of the church. In those days everyone knew where to sit. But as we were leaving, he spoke to me in the aisle. He muttered in a low, casual voice (you know, the voice that says "good sermon" or "nice weather") but his words were, "I loaded two shells with salt."

I don't know if he really did, but we left his melons alone after that for a couple of years. (If you have never lived on a farm in the South, you may be unfamiliar with the practice of replacing the lead shot with ice-cream salt. It is a good, non-lethal way to attract a person's attention.) We did not think he would shoot us. But it did hurt my ego to think that we had been so sloppy and that he'd seen us. I just got in a hurry, missed a detail and looked bad in front of Mr. Crossford, who had told me to not get in hurry and to "do it right."

Egos are special things to 12-year-old boys.

Thirty-eight years later I was reminded of that old lesson. As Pam and I were starting our real estate practice, our broker said that we needed a "farm." I soon found out that this meant a neighborhood in which we would be experts. Our broker was very enthusiastic and said there was nothing to it. We just had to get to know the area and people, and then they would send us business. Sounded easier than planting sweet potatoes and promised to pay better.

Looking back on the broker's advice, I honestly don't know if he thought this was the best thing for us to do, or if he just couldn't think of anything else to say. Over time, I have found that geographic farming is expensive to do correctly; it is not for beginners on limited budgets. The broker had never done it systematically and productively himself, but his mother had and it sounded like a great idea.

To receive the promised huge benefits we were prepared to shell out marketing money and substantial energy before people would send us business. This was our first big marketing project and I was going to make it a success.

Impatient as always, I decided to be very active and visit the 438 homes in our farm. I knocked on doors and handed out brochures, newsletters, and goodwill in general. This was getting way too close to real farm work in its level of effort. But it accomplished the two things I needed most: it generated a bit of business and provided a lot of experience.

My first listing came from this effort. It was a cute little house in great condition. I didn't know enough about the business to realize that the dumpy-looking house next door would hurt our cause, but that's another matter. Sue, the owner, was pretty close on her mortgage so we had to price the house near the top of the market. Sue needed to sell so that she and her husband-to-be could qualify for the loan on their dream house. Sue would live in his house until the new one was built. He lived three blocks away.

After a few disappointments, and more time than I thought it would take, we got a contract. I was so excited. Selling your first listing is a bit like a first date. I was doing everything as properly as I could and hoping to get kissed.

The first thing a listing agent does when he gets an offer on a listed home is work up a net sheet. On this form we list all the costs of sale, any expenses we believe will come up, and the loan balance, and subtract these figures from the offer price to determine the only number the seller cares about: the net proceeds. I filled out my first net sheet in order to make sure the deal would work; Sue did not have any cash. She was as good as her word and would be glad to break even, but she could not take any money to closing. I prorated taxes, figured the homeowner association (HOA) fees, and got the exact payoff from her mortgage company. This was my first net sheet, so it was going to be a piece of work. After double-checking all the numbers I had written, I showed Sue that she would get out clean. Her loan would be paid off, her credit would be clear, and she would be free to go on with the wedding, which, of course, was her over-arching goal.

As a new agent, negotiating repairs and handling lender-required repairs was educational, but not traumatic. I didn't know that on a government-backed loan, like our FHA, if the appraiser sees broken glass (any broken glass) it has to be fixed before the loan goes through. We had a little crack in the corner of a pane on one of the six windows of the garage door. It was only two inches long and did not even leak. I just blew it off. Who could care about a garage door? The Feds do. I ended up doing the repair myself the night before closing, still wearing my coat and tie. The neighbors were amused, and I was in a hurry.

This entire story is a parable about Mr. Crossford, but I did not know that until the next day. Imagine, you have started a new business and after 50 days you are about to get your first commission check—a nice one. I was excited, my bank was excited, my over-burdened credit cards were vibrating.

I was 10 minutes late to the closing.

Have you ever walked into a room and before you heard or even saw anything you just knew that something was very, very wrong? I think of vinegar. Have you ever poured vinegar into fresh sweet milk? It becomes curds and whey immediately. The excitement turned to panic that quickly. *We were $2,800 short to close.* This number had a familiar ring to it. My client could not sign—she did not have cash to close, and worse, I had told her she did not need any. The first thing I did was to check my net sheet. In the time it took for my mouth to fill with cotton, I saw the problem. I had not figured in my commission. I had been in a hurry, gotten sloppy, and made a really dumb mistake. Imagine, dear colleague; I forgot to figure in my commission, my very first commission.

At this point the buyer had his household goods on an Allied van heading for Texas and Sue had a crew hired for later that day to move the "big stuff" to her sweetie's house. At an earlier point in the transaction I would have had a few options; at this point, I only had one. We had to close the deal. Here my story becomes a "we" story because I had to tell Pam what I had done on the net sheet. Of course, she felt worse about how I felt than about the lost commission.

I called my broker and got his permission to give up his part of the commission (60/40 agent/broker split) and I gave up mine. We closed. The credit cards stopped vibrating.

I think this event made me a better agent; I *know* it made me a more careful one. Still, I thought about this mess for months afterward. Possibly a man's ego is not so different from a boy's. I was disappointed in myself for not having learned such an old lesson. The funny part about this is that Sue has done three other deals with us over the last eight years, given us a ton of referrals, and has joined our company as an agent. Her point was that everyone makes mistakes, and she wanted to work with someone who took the blame when it was his turn.

That much-desired $2,800 we lost has come back literally ten-fold, and this does not count the friendships we've made. Doing it right has many variations, I've found, but one quality it always has is of "doing the right thing."

◌

When we found out that we could get referrals from people after we made mistakes, even big ones, it was an eye-opener. Every time we see a problem in a transaction we know it is a referral opportunity in disguise. Not everyone sees tough situations in the same way, and sometimes problems are completely overlooked, as we will see in the next chapter.

9 The Truth is a Matter of Perspective

Or, Your Detail is My Big Deal

This is a short chapter and doesn't cover much. However, just because some important points are quickly made, don't think that they are any less significant. In the Bible we learn that pride goes before a fall; in real estate we learn that taking something for granted goes before a delayed closing. Here, we will discuss some of the key details.

Earlier I mentioned the importance of checklists. Even if a pilot takes off three times a day, she still goes through the checklist before each flight. They are almost that important in real estate. I say almost because we seldom die if a deal crashes, but it hurts a lot. The other problem is perspective. As an agent, I know what I mean with the question, "are you married?" To me it is very simple and it does not require judgment calls or evaluation. It's like pregnancy. No one is a little pregnant. (Still, a couple of years ago we had a client get confused on that one. See the story that follows, "Are You Married?")

The point here is not to say we occasionally get clients who aren't the sharpest knives in the drawer. Rather, we all see things differently. It was not the client's fault that she did not grasp the technical importance of marriage in a community-property state. We continually have to educate our clients and ask questions. Also, we keep in mind the fact that while the client may understand our questions, they often don't understand their own answers.

I have to remind myself all the time that the average person doesn't even know what features he needs in his house. How can he know what the critical elements of information are for loan approval?

This first story sounds like an urban legend: "I know a lady who put her poodle in the microwave to dry it." It isn't. We were there and the got the story from Carlie, the title closer, herself.

Carlie is the most credible title closer we know; she lived this one and Rich tells it.

God Will Provide

My old grandfather loved to sit under his grape arbor and drink, or smoke, or shoot the crows that came looking for his grapes. I suppose that if you ranked people on a nice-ness scale, he would not show up high. To my recollection, no one ever said he was even friendly. But there is more to life than personality. At the unconscionable age of 86, the old guy had lived a lot. He could tell great stories, but to my chagrin, this afternoon he was tending toward the philosophical.

He said, "There is no such thing as bad beer; some is just better than others."

Since no story followed, I was left with that bit of wisdom to ponder. As an eleven-year-old the statement seemed a bit impractical. However, the last 45 years have shown it to be good guidance.

What makes it memorable is its broad application. We speak of bad days, but of course any day that you get to see the end of is not a really bad one. Some, however, are just not as much fun as others, and this particular day in '98 was one of those.

We had spent hours in a closing; nothing seemed to come together as it should. It was one of those closings in which if something was supposed to add up, it didn't; and if it was supposed to be documented, it wasn't. The thing went on and on. We managed to cram 35 minutes of productivity into just over two hours. But even during this mess I felt I was lucky in a couple of ways. We had the best title closer I knew of, Carlie King. We also had very cool clients who let us do our job and only asked pertinent, unemotional questions. That was a big deal; we were fiddling with *their* money.

At the end of the day it all worked out and the deal funded. This is agent-speak for "the buyers got their house keys and the sellers got paid." We were pooped.

III The Closing Celebration

I had only been in the business a couple of years and had never seen a simple-looking closing get so bad.

"Carlie," I asked with that knowledgeable tone only the inexperienced have, "have you ever seen one crazier than this?"

I was being rhetorical and was taken back when she took me literally. She answered my question with a quizzical glance that asked: "Do you really want to hear this?" With bait like that, I bit. Dear colleague, you would have too. I stretched back in the enfolding leather chair as Carlie related a short but amazing story.

The nondescript couple and two average kids arrived at the title company on time for closing. It was an average deal. They were under contract to purchase a $150,000 house in an older neighborhood. The contract was for cash, which was just a bit unusual for that price range. (Usually, cash deals are for more expensive homes.)

The sellers had been elated to get a cash offer; that meant it could close quickly. The husband had already started working at his new job out of state. They jumped at this opportunity to get the family back together. He rented temporary housing in the new city until they got funds from this sale. The husband had put a contract on a new home and it was set to close right after this sale. Things were moving quickly.

The buyer's agent was relatively new, but an okay guy. He had done more than a few deals already. As fate would have it, though, he was only on the cusp of becoming experienced.

When the buyers arrived, Carlie led them and their agent into her office and laid out the closing documents. After going over the settlement sheet, she asked for the cashier's check for the purchase amount. Mr. Buyer looked a bit sheepish and admitted that they did not have the check. Carlie was not one to jump to conclusions or get excited without a "good reason," and she calmly asked him when he *would* have the money.

Mr. Buyer said that they were devout Christians and "took God at His word." At this point, Carlie said, she started to panic. This was "good reason." The story the husband related had all the characteristics of a dream, and it should have been one. The husband's story was that when they were looking at this home, they found a dollar bill in the driveway. This, they said, was God telling them that they were supposed to have this house and that God would provide for it.

"Logically," (this was his interesting choice of word) "we felt that He would get us the money."

Carlie said the room became very quiet. She asked the agent if he had verified funds; he had not.

"These were such fine people, who could question them?"

The air conditioning seemed to stop working and the room instantly felt humid.

Needless to say, the closing didn't happen. The sellers put the house back on the market. The contract on their new one fell through. The buyers went back to la-la land. The buyer's agent knew he was certifiably foolish, and the seller's agent felt fortunate not to be sued. He had violated his fiduciary responsibility by not verifying funds to close before accepting the contract.

While she related this story of her worst closing, I could still see the concern of that past moment cross her face in momentary creases at the mouth and a narrowing of her eyes. Maybe not a bad day—she did see the end of it—but definitely most others are better.

☙

"Are You Married?"

When Rich and I got married, he was still in the Army. Within a month of the "I dos," we were selling the house in Northern Virginia and heading to his new job in Leavenworth, Kansas. He was going to teach at the Army's Command and General Staff College. This was exciting because it gave us the prospect of having regular work hours, weekends off, and not as much traveling. While we were dating, it seemed he was gone half the time, and when he was in town, he was at work. It took me a while to realize that that was the Army officer norm.

As an instructor, Rich felt it was a good idea to have the captains he taught over to our quarters occasionally. He did this partly for the fun of it, since he loves to cook, but also to make certain that they knew how to act when invited to dinner at a field-grade officer's quarters. The three-story 100-year-old house two blocks from headquarters was a bit imposing, and the perfect place for this sort of subtle instruction.

On one occasion, a particularly affable senior captain, Kevin, stayed on after just about everyone else had left. We were sharing stories, and he related an incident common in Washington, DC. The issue was how to tell a valueless detail from a big show-stopping issue. The military makes a big deal of this and Kevin's example was a 21st-century classic.

He had been invited to one those almost-business parties that major contractors host in Washington on a regular basis. The invitation came because of his job, not any friendships, although he knew a lot of people there. The room was well-sized to hold the crowd. Lighting was ample but not glaring, the eats were beautiful, and there was no line at the open bar. He figured that this was already worth the trip. Now he wanted to kick it up a notch. (Not many Army captains have ever watched Emeril Lagasse; I was proud of him. As I recall, Rich went to the refrigerator. He knew where this story was going.)

Being a bachelor, Kevin conducted a recon of the area, which at first looked unusually bleak for a contractor party in DC. However, before long he did notice a classy-looking lady in a black dress, and she knew how to wear it. She was possibly his age or a few years his senior, but nice, and her glass was empty. No ring. They spoke and did the phone-number exchange ritual of singles at a DC party.

After their date two days later, things progressed better than Kevin had even hoped. As she was turning down the comforter, he noticed the picture on the bedroom wall of a Navy captain, a grade equal to an Army full colonel. A grade three levels above Kevin. The voice of reason made him ask a question. His question sounded innocent enough when said it, just in conversation, "Who is the guy in the picture?"

"Oh, he's my ex-husband; he doesn't even come here very much any more. We're sort of separated."

A lot of civilians actually don't understand that military people are governed by a different set of laws than the rest of us. This makes sense when you think about it. In our normal life no one can ever order us to attack an enemy who is trying to kill us. Soldiers live in such a world, and the rules are different and unambiguous. Nothing is "sort of" anything. The military code is particular, and still features a real adultery law. Kevin knew this senior officer could nip his budding career with just a few phone calls.

The immediate problem was that this lady's reply just didn't answer the mail. Kevin really wanted to know if "ex-" meant ex-marriage and she was single, or just "ex-" as in he doesn't live here *much* any more. Visions of the front door opening were already deflating our optimistic Kevin. The story had a few more funny moments after that, but events conspired to develop a terminal case of mood murder.

I thought the guidance Rich gave the captains about bawdy or locker-room stories at dinner parties had more applicability to the military than it would have to real estate. I was wrong.

About four years ago Keri came into our lives.

We had helped her brother buy a house the year before. He was a fun-loving business type who knew what he wanted and loved a good time. Whatever he said he meant. We knew that he had a sister and that she had had some hard times. Rich met her once. When she decided to buy a house, naturally her brother referred her to us.

In my consultation I asked if she was married, the two-year-old playing on the floor begging the question. The answer was an emphatic no with an implied, "next question, please."

With Keri I didn't want to get any deeper into a hurtful part of her past than necessary. Also, and naively, I didn't appreciate the way the world looks at this situation. You see, sometimes the average Joe or Jane can't distinguish "separated" from "divorced." Having the bum out of their life is the point and either status is a great improvement. But the state of Texas has a pretty strong opinion on the issue, and the exact wording matters. It turns out that Keri was actually the average Jane.

If you are married, it doesn't matter if you're separated or married under common law, married means community property in Texas. Until you have a signed, blessed-by-the-court, recorded divorce decree, you're married. Do not pass Go. Without this decree, your soon-to-be-sort-of-ex-spouse has the right to 50% of the property you buy.

Now, most folks in the process of divorce don't think kindly of their soon-to-be ex. Keri was not an exception. We, however, did not know they still had "proceedings" ahead of them. We thought "no" to the question about marriage meant not married. How agents can deceive themselves, dear reader. In this we had company. The lender had gotten the same response and had not followed up on it either.

We found a great house that Keri could afford and that her dad, the cosigner, could qualify for. He was putting in the down payment and some fix-up money too. Things went smoothly until about a week before the scheduled closing. It was the busiest part of summer and the lender, who also saw Keri's two-year-old, remembered to ask if there was a divorce decree. He used the term "if" because it is the twenty-first century. Not everyone with a baby has been married; it is inconvenient, but not unusual. Being rude or overly intrusive was not the point; he needed to do his job. Keri, for her part, had never intended dishonestly. In her mind the guy was gone, not her husband, history. The legal stuff was over her intellectual and emotional horizon, out of sight and mind. When finally asked, she readily admitted that she had married the bum, but he was out of her life.

"I need a copy of the divorce decree," was the statement that stopped the action.

Being still legally married opened a real can of worms.

In these situations, there are recourses, but none of them are fun. The lender requires the soon-to-be ex to sign the deed of trust (because a spouse can't put a lien against a piece of property they both own unless the other spouse is aware of the lien) and the Truth in Lending disclosure. Now, neither of these is a big deal, but they require the presence of the soon-to-be ex at closing. In an ugly divorce case, you're leaving a lot of hope in the hands you're planning to slap if you do this.

The other option is to have the soon-to-be ex sign a specific power of attorney for this piece of property and a special warranty deed giving back his or her part of the property to the spouse buying it. If something must be done, this is my favorite option. The only other way is to get single, then get a house. As an agent who likes predictable closings, I am no fan of going to a closing and having clients practice divorce court. A good closing is a boring closing—no surprises, no drama.

This particular story had a happy ending, though. Because her father had already qualified for the loan, we arranged for him to buy Keri's house. Later, when the divorce dust settled, he could deed the house over to her.

Funny, but now it's easy to add the question, "Have you ever *been* married?" to all our initial consultations.

08

10 Strong Files make Smooth Deals

Or, Don't Invent the Wheel and Go Faster

Organization and systemization have been recurring themes in this book and that isn't going to change. These are the tools of leverage that allow us to give better service and make more money. In the last story you noticed that our buyer presentation had a weak spot: we did not get into enough detail on marital status. The reason for this is simple. Before we get into the house-hunting process, we make sure our buyer clients get into the loan process. Lenders normally handle this up front because the divorce decree is needed for underwriting the loan. Our position was that if the underwriter is happy, everybody is happy. But our system was not foolproof; now it is better. I used the word better because no system is foolproof.

How we developed our homebuyer system is a process any new agent should consider. At a coaching event in Denver years ago, we met an agent with a buyer book. It was beautiful, with a plastic see-though cover and color on most pages. The book had market-area notes and covered state requirements for disclosure. This agent had integrated his buyer book into his dialogs and presentation techniques. At various times while showing homes and during the contract-to-closing period he went back to it. The home-buying process was now visible to his clients. *We appropriated his system whole.* Of course I had to change a few of the pages and dialogs because Texas is not California, where he was from, but that was easy. It was the concept that was hard.

With minimal work, we had a tested and proven model that systemized consistency in the home-buying process. This is important for two income-oriented reasons. First, a good presentation does not do anyone any good and will not add a cent to the bottom line if it is not professionally and consistently used. I get paid for what I do, not what I plan to do. Here was a tool that covered the issues correctly every time. The printed page never forgets or gets in a hurry. I just pick a copy of the booklet off the shelf in the office and I'm ready to present.

Visibility is referability

The second big benefit of the system, after being consistent, is that it is visible. Remember the point a few pages back about referability. For me to be referable I have to do two things: give good service and convey to my clients that anyone referred to us will get *the same quality treatment—every time.* Conveying this concept is difficult because the home-buying process is intangible for the most part. "He could select interesting houses," or "She could show houses well," are not the same as, "He fixed my transmission for only sixteen hundred dollars." Transmissions and money are absolutes, and easily quantifiable. But a tool like the buyer book provides some substance to our nebulous process. When this is coupled with the regular stay-in-touch system, consistent dialogs, and predictable frequency of mail-outs, clients start to see a trend and feel better about telling their circle of influence about us. This is referability.

This is also the perfect type of system for a real estate practice. I worked on the project during the time I scheduled and it didn't interfere with anything else. When we got an assistant I quickly found out that she did a better job of putting the books together than I did. I could have hired out the job from the beginning. Once one good copy exists the guys at the corner We Copy It store will finish the job. In fact they, or a teenager hired for half a day, will do it better than any average agent. Getting a business-building job done in a manner that does not affect prospecting time, client service, or your other marketing tasks is the goal. This is efficiency.

At this point you should be fired up to go out and steal some good stuff. I don't mean just a buyer book, but filing systems, business organization methods, and even past clients. Put on the mask and gloves and get ready. We are going to discuss where to steal from.

New clients in old files

Start with your broker. She has a very good idea who does the best files. The best is what you want. Years ago I attended a class for agents' assistants in our real estate office. The instructor, one of the assistants for the top producer in the company, showed us how to organize a file. Her system was easy to use and allowed everyone to know where the different documents would be located. This is very critical. Imagine you have ten houses under contract, but not closed yet, and have to check on the status of appraisals, surveys, inspections, repairs, etc. If Rich filed something with this system, I could find it. Technically, we did not steal it because it was offered, but we took it and still use it.

If you can't find a filing system worth stealing in your office, visit your lender. Because of underwriting rules the good ones organize files well. If your lender doesn't organize files well you may need to think about it. The point is not how you organize your files but that they are organized. Believe me, we get calls all the time from clients who closed deals years ago and want to know if I have a copy of some document. With our filing system, I know what I kept and what is dumped after closing.

Let's talk about how to make *money* with files for a paragraph or two. After we got our lead-generation systems up and running, which can take a few years, we had become as busy as we wanted to be. However, it took a couple of years for them to reach full effect; before then, life had some slow minutes. Here we were, Rich and Pam ready to help the world, and the world was not knocking on our door. We knew we were doing what was necessary to build our business long term, but we still wanted more "now" business. The right files are one place to look—the ones in the office bone-yard.

In every line of work some people give it a shot and don't make it. Real estate is like that. The introductory story to this book is typical of too many people. Jane Doeson did do some business and had some clients. Her files are called orphans in the business because she is not around to help those clients any more. Guess what; these human beings know the name of your company and probably feel good about it. Check with your broker and adopt some of these people. The situation in most areas is that buyers are ready to move (or have to relocate) between three and five years after a home purchase.

If you have some slow time in the middle of the day, you have two options. You can go to lunch with an agent friend and talk about your troubles or hear about her uncommitted clients. This seems to be the popular one. On the other hand, you could do some prospecting, such as adopting some buyers from the five-year-old orphan files in the office. Why not help people and make money?

More dialoging for dollars

Select files in the price range you want to work in that closed three to five years ago. Make yourself a call list and get these people on the phone. The dialog is simple. Don't make it complicated. Just call the homeowners and introduce yourself.

"Hi, I'm Pam O'Bryant from ABC Realty. Our records show that you worked with Jane Doeson a few years back to purchase your new home. Jane is no longer with us and we want to make sure all of our clients get the help they deserve. Is this a good time for me to update our records?"

If the answer is no, then use the alternative appointment close: "Would this evening at six-thirty be okay to call back, or would tomorrow after nine be better?"

If the answer is yes, then get into a conversation. You want to know two important things about the person. First, do they or their friends need any real estate help now, and second, is this person a candidate for your database? After four or five years most people will be selling soon. If you have to send them a couple of mailings a month for a year to earn $4,000 in commission, oh well. Life is hard, isn't it?

You may be thinking that you don't stand a chance of getting those old orphan files. They are such an obvious source of now or nearly-now business that there is a line outside the file room. Never fear. Remember, Jane never went into the file room. She was average and went to lunch with an agent friend. Just for the record, Rich and I don't have anything against agents or socializing with them, but it is a fact that during the work day our job is lead generation, unless we are actually working with a client. You will get few leads from your fellow agents in the office. If you must eat with someone, meet a past client and deepen the relationship or lunch with some businessperson who is in a position to influence a lot of people. You only stop generating leads when you have enough of them, and when is that? Of course, check with your office manager and be sure to understand all the local and state rules involved before you grab a bunch of files and start calling.

In this next story having a good file was key to handling my client's fear and keeping our sanity. Most of the people we work with are basically good people and try their best, and I am describing both sides of the average deal, not just our clients. The buyer in this case may have been an all-right guy on some level. However, as a human, he could not trust or respect anyone. He honestly believed that everyone was out to take advantage of everyone else. These sorts of people feel justified in doing anything to anyone. As Rich's cranky old grandfather would have said, "They need watchin'."

Inspections Are a Pain

The view from our patio is beautifully limited by a couple of ancient oak trees. The large, almost symmetrical, limbs restrict our view with a natural lattice that seems different every day, but always looks serene. Rich and I sit out there many evenings after work with a glass of wine. Romantics would read poetry in such a spot; being agents, we discuss our worst problems in this best of places. I've often wondered how this habit got started.

The other day I stayed true to the pattern. The issue was a favorite old gripe, repairs. One of our listings was under contract and the buyer's inspector found the bricks over a window had bowed out. This is a problem. We were doing the engineer reports and dogging the builder. The house was only six years old and I think it's a construction problem. Rich figures it will all work out. When it comes to pushing a client's issue, he usually gets it worked out in the end.

The last thing one of our sellers wants is to have problems come up after closing. When Rich alluded to wanting to get this one put to bed, I knew what he was thinking about.

He was referring to the infamous leaking shower pan of the Crumb's house. This was one of those deals that should have been easy. But the inspection got messed up and caused no end of recurring problems.

The house was one of those solid 25-year-old two-stories. It had a nice front yard with good trees, but a very steep back yard. The original owners, the current owner's parents, had done the obvious thing to stabilize it. They built terraces. On these they installed strikingly beautiful flower gardens. Our young client and his wife had inherited the house from his parents and they loved it. But his job had moved to Austin, and driving 90 miles every day had gotten old after a few weeks, and he had been doing it for 17 months. For sanity's sake (his wife's) he had to relocate.

As I have said before, buyers like homes that they can just move into. This was one of those and it sold quickly. The buyer's agent seemed just out of the loop and not very quick. Some agents think that once the contract is accepted they can move on and forget the transaction until the check comes in. These guys don't get as many checks as they could get, and they never get referrals from clients during the home-buying process. How could they? They're afraid to talk to their clients because they don't know what is going on with the transaction.

Rich had to prod to get her to discuss the inspection process with the buyer. Now, Bill the buyer was a special case from the beginning. Of course, we expect a certain amount of weirdness from people during the negotiation process. There are a few sorts that believe implying a God complex helps them to get a better outcome, more money, or better terms. So we always overlook any rudeness. I had priced the house very optimistically and it looked as though neither Bill nor his agent knew how to question comparable sales. After a bunch of noise, they agreed to a very nice price—for my client. This was our goal. The haggling was not my problem, and generally people are good at heart and get over themselves after the negotiations end. But Bill did not get over it, *ever*.

For inspections, Bill the buyer said he was going to have some friends in the trades come over and check out the house. I was told that they work with this stuff every day and know what they are talking about better than an expensive real estate inspector who "could not change out a hose bib." I expressed my reservations about that and told him he would have to sign a statement saying he waived inspecting the house. This went over, but not well.

An inspection date was agreed to and Rich arrived early. He was concerned that Bill's buddies would damage the house or do something dumb. His only other experience with trades people acting as inspectors ended up with him asking the guys to get off my client's roof and leave. Since they were already out to lunch, Rich figured they might as well go there.

As it turned out on this inspection, only the buyer and his eight-year-old daughter showed up. After 30 aggravating minutes of walking around, they left saying it looked "okay."

The buyer said he wanted to buy the seller's huge cedar-post bed. I suggested to the sellers that he was a flake and I didn't want to complicate the deal by adding this to the contract. They reminded me that the bed had to be taken completely apart to get it out of the house and that "the damn thing weighs over 600 pounds." They agreed to work the deal out with him themselves.

My guys did not get any money up front on the bed, a serious mistake, and they paid for it. The day before closing, Big Bill backed out on the bed deal and demanded that the bed be removed before closing. The poor sellers had to jump through hoops to get it out at the last minute. Bill the buyer was on a roll. Only after several more emotional tiffs did the guy finally close, just a few days late. The sellers moved to Austin, and we thought it was finished.

Bill threatened to sue on the first phone call, two days after closing. He claimed the shower pan was leaking, that we knew about it, and he had been deceived. Rich asked if he really meant deceived, since Rich didn't think Bill knew a word that long. As luck would have it, Rich had gone to the house just three days before closing to get some document signed. The seller had just gotten out of the upstairs shower. The bathroom was still steamy and nothing was leaking. However, we remembered the air handler for the air conditioner was next to the bathroom. The condensation line could have been stopped up and that would cause the sort of leak that Bill described. He admitted that the leak continued even during the day when no one was home. Rich figured there could be a poltergeist showering during the daytime or the A/C condensate line might need to be cleared out, and gave him those options. Bill didn't blow his gasket until Rich suggested that he read over his inspection report to see if the A/C system had been checked. This was not the politic thing to say, but Big Bill was having another fit anyway, so Rich figured he might as well have some fun.

Rich did talk him out of trying to fix the shower pan until he had a professional check the A/C line. If Bill fixed it, we knew we *would* have a shower pan problem.

During the course of the following year I got an occasional badgering call, but nothing of note. Then the letter from the lawyer arrived. Big Bill was claiming that the foundation had failed, that I had known it, and that he had been deceived yet again. I think "deceived" was a favorite word or the only impressive one he knew. We had to ask ourselves the two obvious questions: Was it really broken? And when did it break? Well, being a normally nosy person anyway (Rich calls it inquisitive), I drove over to the house. Out of habit, I took the digital camera; and this is a great habit to have. The place was a wreck. The gardens looked bombed out and the grass on the west side of the house was totally brown, while the shady east side had a lot of green in it yet. This was important to know.

There are two common ways to break a concrete foundation without having any mechanical problems with the house. The first is to fail to water the soil around the house so that the soil contracts and moves away from the foundation. This leaves the moist earth under the middle of the house higher than the perimeter so that the outside beam of the slab breaks away. The other way is to have uneven moisture around the house. Here the low, dry side cracks off and drops down. Now both of these conditions are easily avoided. Just keep the grass the same color all the way around the house, and make sure that color is green.

I had saved the pictures we made to market the house the year before and now I had the comparison pictures. We sent them along with a nice letter to his attorney. I suggested that his client may or may not have a problem with his foundation, but if he did he himself caused it, and to please not bother us until they had an engineer's report to discuss. I attached a copy of the signed waiver of inspection for good measure. Then we used the old stonewall approach that didn't work so well for Mr. Nixon in '75.

I should mention that the sellers also got a couple of high-priced-lawyer letters. We kept them in the loop and sent them copies of everything we did on their behalf. The effect was to strengthen our relationship with them.

This was a time-consuming problem and did cause some well-founded concern for the sellers and us. But how could we avoid it in the future? No law requires a Bill or Bubba to get a mechanical inspection of a house before purchase. Of course, 99% of all buyers have basic common sense. They gladly spend $200 to avoid making a $120,000 mistake and buying a home that is not structurally sound. But the Bills and Bubbas are still out there. The young sellers asked us to sell another property for their family the next year. Too bad they are staying in Austin.

All I can say is that the oak trees are still beautiful off our patio. Yesterday, Rich had two cases of wine delivered to the house, so we will continue to ponder.

ଓ

The story you just finished described how a poorly represented immature person could make life difficult if you don't have your deal documented. I'm certain that when Buyer Bill's attorney saw that his client had declined an inspection *in writing*, he lost interest. In this next story, I'm not sure what the real answer is. I don't get to control the loan programs. More importantly, my understanding of the agent's job is that I'm suppose to help my clients do what they want to do as long as it is not illegal, immoral, or fattening. See what you think.

Some People Aren't Ready to Own a Home

I can still remember how it felt the day I drove by Tommy and Sharon's new house. The shocker was seeing a for-sale sign in their yard. The house was vacant, they had already moved, and I hadn't even known! I was hurt. To think after all we'd been through together to get them into a house, their very first house, that they would sell it without even telling us. They'd bought it less than a year before! How could they have moved already? After the shock, I noticed that things just did not add up.

True, I didn't stay in touch as well as I could have. We didn't have them on our regular follow-up system, because we didn't want to expand our database in that price range. I had sent them a few cards, and I believed in my heart that they thought of me as their real-estate person. But now they'd moved and I hadn't known about it. I even called Rich and asked if he had gotten a call. This is not implying that husbands ever fail to pass along messages. I was just checking.

I did some investigating after that. Turns out the house went into foreclosure. My cute young couple lost everything, including what little good credit they had managed to salvage from previous disasters.

But let me start from the beginning.

At the weekly real-estate marketing meeting at the office, a speaker, Larry the lender, told us about a new down-payment assistance program. He said it was a better idea than sliced bread and slicker than butter on a doorknob. This was several years ago, before these programs became a dime a dozen. His program seemed very liberal, but was in line with HUD's goal of getting more lower-income people into homes. To make this stunt work, a non-profit organization acted as a middleman between the seller and buyer. It collected 4% of the sales price from the seller and gave 3% to the buyer for a down payment. The non-profit profited by 1% on the deal for doing nothing but moving two pieces of paper around and having a bank account. Someone was making money and it wasn't the principals. Still, it allowed a buyer to get into a house with no down payment out of pocket, just a higher mortgage payment. This was because the seller would up the sales price by 4% to cover her "gift" to the non-profit organization. Larry the lender said they used appraisers who were more liberal than most, because of the higher sales price needed to cover the 4% donation to the non-profit. This was news to me; I had doubted appraisers even voted, much less knew what liberal meant!

I was a little skeptical, but we had just met Tommy and Sharon and they really, really wanted a home of their own. They had the cutest little three-year-old and they wanted her to have a yard to play in where they could feel she was safe. They both had pretty good jobs, but their credit was not in the best of shape; actually, they had too much schooling and not enough bill paying. And they had almost no money. Once I saw that little girl's face, however, I knew I had to find a way to get them into a home. Anyway, the lender said it was HUD's position that when poor people moved into a home of their own, they would learn to budget their money. Doesn't everyone?

I set Tommy and Sharon up to visit with Larry. He said they

were a little shaky, but he thought he could get it done. The interest rate wouldn't be the best, because of their less-than-stellar credit history, but the deal could get done as long as Rich and I could find a seller willing to make the contribution. We could do that.

It was a cute little house on a quiet street, just barely in their budget. I talked the seller into the contribution, and then hoped that Larry actually had a liberal appraiser who could help us out on the sales price. The guy turned out to be a liberal to the left of Lenin, going by his appraisal; his bumper sticker said, "I vote NRA." Go figure.

By the time we had rolled in all the costs the kids couldn't pay, the sales price was almost 7% over the market value for the neighborhood. Mr. I vote NRA appraised it for the full contract price. This program was slick.

Larry managed to get the loan squeaked through at a little more than half a percent higher than the going rate. As we had warned, the payment would be tough, but they were committed to buying a home. Anyway, we reminded ourselves, people learn to budget when they become homeowners, right? HUD said so.

We proceeded to the closing celebration.

The day they moved in, I stopped by with pizzas and met the whole family. They must have had 20 people there. Everyone was impressed that the young couple could own their own home. To most of the family, setting up a new home meant removing the wheels. The majority of the family still rented, including one set of parents. I cashed my commission check and went home, pleased to have been able to help yet another family achieve the American Dream. Rich and I moved on to the next client. It wasn't until I drove by the house that day that I really thought about them again.

Turns out Sharon's hours had been cut back right after closing, and fate decided to play more games with them. The baby got sick and the car broke down. Here was mom on reduced hours, taking even more time off with the child, and they didn't have enough money to both fix the car and make the house payment. One thing led to another, and before they could look up, they were three months behind on house payments. The hill looked too steep to climb. They didn't know what to do, and were too embarrassed to call me or any other professional for help. The only people they consulted were family members, and from what I had briefly seen, none of them could manage money either.

They just "let the house go back." Since their credit was already not so great, they didn't figure that this would make much difference. Little did they know that that little girl of theirs could be stuck living in apartments for years. Foreclosures kill your chances of buying a home for a long time, unless you can save up a big down payment.

I've thought a lot about this couple lately. I've had other families come into my office having heard about how they can get into a house with no money. Sometimes I tell them I can't help them.

ଔ

11 Keep Your Head and Commission

Or, If the Client Goes Over the Edge, Don't Follow

Keeping current on transactions while they are in progress is key for a lot of reasons, one of which we have not mentioned. What we have discussed is the need to stay up to date so that you get the information needed to close. Another fabulous reason is to establish myself in the client's mind as their agent for life. This gets referrals. These are great reasons; you can't beat closing deals and referrals as a good way to spend time. But the next reason is more subtle: fear management.

Some transactions are just weird; some clients act that way. If you have a regular stay-in-touch program, such as our Tuesday-update calls, you will get to know about a lot of problems early enough to handle them before they get out of hand. That is, before the agent on the other side of the deal finds out about it and the deal gets in jeopardy. I am not recommending lying to or hiding stuff from the other agent that she has a right to know. However, I am saying it is always best to solve problems with as little uncontrolled visibility as possible. To put it bluntly, if my client does something dumb, I want to find out about it first. Embarrassment in real estate is when the other agent calls me to tell me about my own client.

When some negative event occurs during the course of moving from listing the house to closing the deal that will distress my client, my first reaction is to figure out how to manage their fear. In an ideal situation I will find out about the problem before the client does. This is usually the way it happens because we stay in touch with all the parties on a regular basis. Once identified, I go into problem-solving mode. What I do is work out a solution to the difficulty, or a course of action that will probably fix it. Then I call the client and manage the problem for them. This is controlled visibility and here is how to manage the problem: I explain the difficulty, and then I make it as bad as it could be—blow it up. Then provide the resolution. Some problems don't resolve quickly and in those cases I still call the client. Remember this rule: bad news is going to get to them whether I call or not. The next rule is that problems are not wine and will not get better with age. Even if I cannot solve a problem, if I discuss it, I can make certain that the facts are related clearly and explained professionally. (See Dialoging for Dollars in Chapter 8.)

This is the communication that positions me as the consultant. Consultants control information, and through their advice, they manage situations. My job is to manage the fear that problems generate. Remember that when we started the relationship, I told the clients they would have turbulence, and I have reminded the clients of this several times. Some transactions just go like clockwork; in fact, most do. However, one thing you can count on, no client will ever say, "It went too smoothly; I wish we had had more problems." However, if you promise a completely smooth transaction, you are setting yourself up to disappoint your client.

Stay informed, stay in touch, and take immediate action on all problems.

Why they sell

Unfortunately, this isn't all there is to it. Behind almost every basket-case client is a bucketful of problems. We have all read the statistics that a divorce is emotionally equal to a death in the family or moving out of town. Every few months a popular magazine runs an article on stressors in modern life and restates this. Just how disturbing it is depends on a lot of things. Mostly, it depends on the person. Everyone is unique, and we all have a blow-up point where we lose it. But this point is different with different people and in different situations.

Powder kegs and sparks

Moving is very stressful all by itself, but think about why people move. Some of the most common reasons are not fun all by themselves, even without real estate hassles. Divorce is very popular, because by splitting up the incomes, neither party can afford the house any more. The downsizing caused by the death of a spouse is another. In San Antonio, with its several military bases, relocation to a new job is at or near the top of everyone's list. What all of this means is that for many clients their emotional plate is full before I ever get involved. These guys are powder kegs, and their life situation is giving off sparks.

One afternoon comes to mind. Rich and I went to a listing appointment, and we knew in advance that the owners were getting a divorce. The clients did not know that we knew this and had decided not to tell us. That would have been all right with us, but they had not agreed on anything else, such as to get along with each other in our presence. Here were two people saying polite things to each other in the most contradictory way possible. Once I looked over at Rich and thought he was going to lose it—*laughing*. I quickly changed the subject, and we got the listing. They never brought up the divorce. Eventually, the attorneys started to call and the cat was out.

I mention this because in the middle of a transaction, I tend to focus on the real-estate issues. Of course that is what is expected, but I still have to be attuned to the client's world. During the update calls, *ramble time* is important. I throw out a few fishing questions just to check on the temperature of the water. If the husband has left for the new job in DC, I ask about his living arrangements or the new job. If I have referred an agent to them in DC, I want to know how the house hunting is going. After these questions, I try to get just a minute of general "how do you feel?" time. I mean it when I say just a minute. Some clients, particularly the needy ones, are happy to talk all afternoon. If I let them keep me on the phone, not only do I waste time, but also I hurt our relationship. This is an important point.

Don't be a friend

When a client is stressed, that is the time she needs me to be strong and provide leadership. The client has friends, but friends can't solve problems and I can. Clients may sound like they want you to be friendly and cuddly, but that is just their behavior pattern. They will value me if I stay in my role and remain the trusted consultant providing options and managing the process.

These next two stories are fun to read. Also, they hit the points we have discussed right on the head. Rich and I lived through the first one together, but he had all the fun in the second one. Even as I tell this first story years later, I still can't believe some of these things happened. Who would have thought it?

Money does not Equal Taste—or Good Sense!

We have a good friend who loves horses, Crown Royal whisky, and a good time; not necessarily in that order. I'll call him Scott. His other traits include being a hard worker and honest to a fault, which taken together makes for a good friend of a decidedly Texas variety. We were having a few beers at a local dance hall and he commented on a friend of his who had a "big house." It did sound impressive. Over 5,000 square feet and it cost over half a million—yep, it sounded impressive. Scott is not one to talk over a friend's personal possessions in public just for the heck of it. His point was that he felt sorry for her.

"Here is a lady, Pam, with all the money she can use, good looking, skinny—and yet she is just not happy."

It seems her marriage was a mess and personally she just could not get it together. While I understand this, I am always amazed at the percentage of people who have six-digit incomes and a net worth in eight digits who are not leading satisfying lives.

It was an interesting story, but our conversation moved on. However, a few months later Scott called me and asked if we would mind calling a friend who was getting a divorce and needed to sell "their" house. I made the call and set up the appointment to list the big house. Scott said not to mention the divorce. The guy knew how people worked.

As always, listing a very complicated large house is interesting. However, spending a couple of hours with two people, Dave and Darlene, who did not like each other but were not going to admit to us that anything was wrong, was a real trip.

Not all trips are fun.

They would not discuss why they were selling the house or their future plans. The divorce sat in the corner where the 300-pound gorilla usually sits. Dave sat at the table imitating the gorilla, and Darlene showed us the house, almost bouncing from room to room. It was a huge, expensive, and very custom home. In several places it seemed the floor plan had lost its way. As I looked quizzically at the odd placement of three doors in the upstairs family room, Darlene boasted that the architect had made a mistake and she had corrected the floor plan.

At times keeping a poker face is as tough as it is necessary.

This was the classic American rich guy syndrome at work. The Mister was a salesperson, a hard worker from the east side, and she was from the same background and a science teacher in a public high school. Together, they had saved money and bought a franchise restaurant, then two, then 20. With their money, she felt that she had good taste and sound judgment on all matters. To her, rich people had good taste—it came with the money. Rich people could afford the best stuff and if you got enough of the best that money could buy, it had to be in good taste. We could see why they did not get along. But that was not my business.

Colleague, when you make the big bucks remember who you are. As a science teacher from the east side, she did not have the experience to design or decorate a $600,000 house effectively or efficiently. That is why we hire professionals. Their architect, a big name guy, knew where to put the doors and closets. The interior design lady had good ideas about colors and coverings. As we wandered from one expensive out-of-place item to the next, it became evident why they thought their house was worth $100,000 more than I did. They had spent that much to make it look bad! The pink and gray marble floors were bad enough, but she had the stuff going through the entry way and into the formal living room and *up* one of the walls around the beautiful granite fireplace. Imagine sky gray and pink marble tiles next to steel-gray and black granite. It hurt my head.

We could go into the 18 other items (purple wallpaper, $700 maroon toilets), but you get the point. Needless to say, we had our challenges finding a buyer, but after four long months it sold. Their relationship had deteriorated by then to the point that the husband did not even come to town any more and I had gotten to know her fireman boyfriend pretty well. He was a sensible guy who did what he was told.

Here is the point: don't take anything for granted. Just because the contract is for over half a million, don't think the clients will not do weird stuff. When people spend more time talking to their attorneys than their spouses, their emotional plate is full. This is when the sparks start to land.

I walked through the house a couple of days before the buyer's final walk-through and saw that the fireplace fake logs were gone. When I asked where they had gone, she said that her father had given them to her and she was taking them. That was a new one: keepsake fireplace logs. Given the deep emotional attachment she had, pointing out that the contract they signed said the logs stayed just did not register. In fact, I felt *I* was not registering. You know the feeling you get when it hits you that the other party has mentally hung up and you've actually been discussing major issues with the phone circuits. I told Rich about the problem, and he did what every macho not-going-to-be-pushed-around agent does. He went to Home Depot and bought a set of fireplace logs. With $17,000 in commissions and closing due in three days, I can afford $150 worth of logs.

Now I was set. The repairs were finished, one owner moved in with boyfriend, other owner out of state with his girlfriend, and the house clean. Then the real-estate gods said, "Not so fast, Pam."

The day before closing, 15 minutes after the buyers were to start their walk-through, I get The Call. The buyer's agent,

Bobbie, one of those respected older agents who has seen it all and knows the business well, was on the line and hot. Not just aggravated, but as we would say in East Texas, pissed off. From her tone I could tell the problem was not just anger; she had been embarrassed, and I was a party to it. If she had not been such a solid, professional agent I would not have believed the comment that followed. Remember, I was taken back by the fact that someone would claim to be attached to fake fireplace logs. Bobbie said my client had sent her handyman into the house and he was changing out the upgraded light switches, all six of them.

Picture this, it's a hoot: a 60ish red-headed agent with the overweight president of a large company and his wife walking through their new executive home. In the middle of the hall is a guy in blue jeans and boots taking light switches out of the wall. It must have been a magic moment.

At this point I figured my client had just gone over the edge. I didn't even call her. I got the make and model of the switches from the handyman and had my electrician install new ones that evening. We were absolutely going to close on time and without any issues. And we did.

In my career as an agent, only twice have clients responded to a survey by saying I was "not helpful" or "just average" at closing. This was the "not helpful." And, sad to say, she was right. The problems they had were profound and the real-estate part was insignificant. I wasn't much help. But I will always remember Bobbie's call: "Pam, they are taking the light switches; what are you going to do about it?" We live for such moments.

Just to close the loop, Bobbie, a true professional, hooked her buyers up with a good interior designer and they got the pink and gray marble out before moving in. After cooling off a while, Darlene has called me several times about real-estate issues and seems much happier now that she is in a smaller home and has a regular life again. She was still with the fireman last time we spoke and her emotional plate had a lot less on it.

೦ಽ

Scorpion in the Bathtub

In the middle of Texas, in the middle of summer, in the middle of morning it is hot. It doesn't just get hot with plain old heat, it's with no breeze and penetrating moisture. The heat is like a cover. Not the smooth cover of a silk sheet on a spring morning or the fuzzy nest of a flannel sheet on a fall night. No, this is a special cover. It is like a sandy sheet of black plastic at the coast. This was the claustrophobic heat on the morning we took Stavenski's wife to see her new home for the first time, hot and itchy.

I've been an agent for eight years and had seen it all, as they say. I had seen the befuddled husband who didn't know his wife nearly as well as he'd thought. And on this hot morning I had the sinking feeling that I was seeing another one. The wife made a slight movement in the second-row captain seat of the van, an almost imperceptible nervous movement, as we slowed down in front of the house. I've seen clients lean forward in anticipation, or sit up straight to see better because of heightened interest, but Stavenski's wife had the head position of clenched nerves and the deepening crease at her mouth that let me know that fun was not on the way. This was an early stage of what behaviorists call fight or flight response, and her expression betrayed the first option.

I braced for a long morning.

Stavenski knew his wife well enough to sense something amiss as we walked up the sidewalk. His perceptive abilities did not extend to understanding the situation, and I could tell he would be caught unprepared by whatever happened. This was sad. And at this critical juncture he did what comes naturally, he made it worse. His wife did not need help in getting aggravated even on a good day. What possessed him at that moment to confess that he had not had the utilities turned on, we will never know. But he did succeed in giving her a good 45 seconds extra to get in a bad mood about the hot, humid house we were about to enter.

With a sinking heart, I fumbled with the lock box.

It always surprises me how much worse paint looks in an empty house than it did when the furniture was there. This empty one looked rough. We got through the living room on just the utility screw-up and how hot the house was. The paint issue didn't surface until we entered the master bedroom, which she pronounced to be in an "illogical place," outside the flow of the house. I started to comment that they may not want a lot of flow through their bedroom, but decided against it. In any case, I didn't have any more idea what an illogical place meant than Stavenski did.

The floor plan was a side issue. We were building up to a full-blown fit of anger laced artfully with feminine victimization, not architectural criticism. However, Stavenski could take it and Stavenski's wife could dish it out; this was their system. They had been married 11 years, so I figured he was probably used to screwing up and getting chewed on by now. But I was caught flat-footed as we made the fateful turn into the bathroom.

Now before we turn that corner in my story and I am forced to re-feel the heat, the itch, language, and other unsavory stuff, I need to explain something about scorpions.

Not everyone is familiar with these creatures in fact, most people know next to nothing about them. Of course, most people are happy with this state of affairs and do not consider their education deficient in that way. But the point is they are not insects. Insects can connote dirtiness, as roaches do, or cause fearful respect, like wasps. But creepy arachnids can do both, and bring a particular crawl-between-your-sheets element of sinisterness with them that touches some people profoundly. Stavenski's wife was subject to this touch.

I suppose, looking back, things would not have gotten out of hand if it had not been a female scorpion. This large beast had about 15 baby scorpions on her back. But, dear colleague, we will get to this; let's return to our story.

Stavenski's wife led the way into the master bath. The sinks were okay, but nothing to write home about. The shower was small and, "why don't people build them with a seat; don't they know women need a seat?" Of course, builders aren't people in the strictest sense of the word, but this was not the time for a flippant comment, no matter how pithy. Unavoidably, and now it seems even fatefully, she came to the big garden tub, the feature that was supposed to save Stavenski's bacon. The woman loved big tubs—he was positive.

Of course the large scorpion was in the tub. When fate has us in a grip she often gives a memorable squeeze just for fun. This gross beast of a female arachnid was not only in the process of increasing her creepy population, but she was eating one of her own young.

Stavenski's wife sputtered; it sounded like a small gas-powered airplane running out of fuel in mid-flight. She wavered. Then she came back at us. Stavenski caught her before she hit the floor, and looked even worse than she did.

Once we were out of the house and under the oak trees it was okay.

This tale could have many chapters, but you can imagine them without me taking up the time. We answered the 100 questions. No, a scorpion is not grounds to go back to the title company. Yes we can get the house painted ("any color you want, dear"). What other beasts does Texas have, and so on.

I am a person who believes people act in what they perceive as their best interests, and on some level Stavenski's wife was such a person. Her best interest was to ensure her place in their relationship. She was top dog and used that scorpion to put her husband back in the box. Her high-pressure executive job had prevented her from doing the house hunting, and there was nothing she could do about that. But taking a couple of unaccompanied trips to the new town and picking the house out by himself combined to be just a bit too much leash for a husband of hers. He needed a lesson. Heel, boy!

Dear colleague, at this point I am supposed to make the observation that, if properly applied, will preclude you from making my mistakes. Experiencing the discomfort of getting a woman 30 pounds north of fighting weight out of a steamy house and going through the resultant grilling are to be avoided. In that vein, I will suggest that you always check a house out before letting your clients in it. Get there first and tell them about any problems before they find them. Don't let them discover the issues themselves if you can help it. This includes inspections and walk-throughs. It really helps to tell the clients the carpet is wet before they get wet shoes. (This was another story, but it happened.)

However, in the big picture often there is no helping it. This is one of the joys of real estate for the well-adjusted agent. Those sad souls in the profession who do not appreciate the vagaries of human nature are destined to be unhappy much of the time. Life just is. The Stavenskis were normal dysfunctional people like most of us. They were both smart and had very productive jobs, which meant, among other things, that they can afford to buy a nice house. It also meant that they come, like every other client, as they are. When we help clients buy a home we see them under stress and out of their comfort zone. The new experience does that for most people. For me, it is people-watching at its best.

We have fully recovered from this event and have become friends. When neither one is under stress they are fun people, like most of us. They come to client parties at least twice a year and send us referrals. Life is good…and interesting.

ଔ

IV The Lead Machine

Or, Building a Business That Feeds You and Your Goals

Building a business is the goal. It's our goal, and it's probably yours, too. However, we really haven't discussed what a business is and how you build one in real estate. Rich and I have done it, and I can explain what we did and why we did it. This isn't an airy-fairy theoretical approach to the topic, but rather a doable approach, because we did it.

Here is what we know.

A business is a systemized activity that can be repeated over and over, typically for financial advantage. My business can be making shoes. If I make enough shoes and people buy them at good enough prices, my business can grow and become a success. Real estate is just like making shoes. (I warned you this was not high theory.)

12 There Are Only Six Ways to Make Money

Or, Pick Two, Only Two

Any way you cut it, there are only six ways to make money as an agent: open houses, For Sale By Owners, geographical farms, general marketing (running ads), Circle of Influence (COI), and business relationships. These can be split into any number of smaller categories, but they are the major ones. It is important to know something about each of them. We checked into them our first 15 months in the business and tried most of them, which was a colossal waste of time, for the most part.

I know this sounds counterintuitive.

Logic would say that the more methods you employ to get quality leads the more business you would get. The problem is that life, or at least real estate, does not work that way. After some months of bum-fuzzling around, we went to an all-day training event at our Board of Realtors. The trainer said a great many things, and most were good, but one point he made stuck with us. He said most agents who don't make it in this business have never gotten properly focused. He listed the above six ways to make money and said that if an agent tried to do three or more of them he would fail, but if he focused on two he was on the path to success. Learn to do two strategies, he preached, at the mastery level and "you will make a six-digit income." That struck a chord with us, and we found that it works.

Heart valves and focus

The point is focus. No one can really understand a lot of things deeply. A while back Rich was watching TV. He seldom watches the thing, so I stopped to see what he was looking at. Dr. DeBakey, the most famous heart surgeon on the planet, was doing some operations and Rich was mesmerized. The doctor did three of them as we watched. They were all the same: heart valves. The guy does 15 to 17 operations a day when he operates. He doesn't open the patient's chest or sew up the patient, he just does the tricky part. The other doctors on the team make good livings, but the big guy makes the big bucks and gets the glory. This was focus.

We were ready for focus after we heard this trainer. We had started a geographical farm, which proved expensive to maintain. We had called on businesses, but not consistently. Now it was time to get a focus and get some income.

We knew we were good in relationship building, so the COI looked appealing, but the problem was that it is a slow starter. While the database could feed us eventually, it could not help with next month's house payment. This observation got us interested in open houses. We had our two strategies. The rest is history.

As luck would have it, my brother, a commercial broker in Cleveland, recommended a coach who specializes in COI development and getting referrals systematically, Joe Stumpf. We attended his training and signed up for coaching. At this point, we were about out of money and put the coaching fees on the credit card. We knew we could do this business.

Training focus

When we got this level of focus, two critical things happened. Most importantly, the task of learning got manageable. With only two strategies to consider, we had the time to become experts on them. The second thing was we started to make some real money.

Once we had focus, we could stop going to every training event in town and just learn what we needed to know. This narrowing of interest helped us spend our time more wisely. This isn't the whole story of the real estate industry but it is where the successful people *start*.

I focus on the things we actually did to build our business but what we did is not the only path. The best example is FSBOs. Neither Rich nor I have ever been interested in working with these people. I don't think this makes us lazy or narrow or immoral. They are just not our cup of tea. However, another agent in our office, a guy who always sells a few more houses than we do annually, works only with FSBOs. He has time-blocked certain hours every workday to call people, and he uses a set script. Don't try to interrupt Tom during call time. He will not respond. After he gets his appointments set up, he goofs off, goes to lunch with anyone, whatever he wants. If he does not have the target number of appointments, he stays with it until he does.

He and I have discussed his strategy and I have suggested building a database and touch programs, but to no avail. This process just does not interest him. While working for a client Tom works very hard to sell the house for the best price. However, after closing he mentally needs to say "next!" and move on.

With experience, we get to know how our strategies work. Tom knows that he will get two listings for every three appointments. Of every five homes he lists, he sells four. So if he sets up nine appointments a month he will close, on average, five homes. An important factor in this sort of practice is that he gets to pick who he calls. This controls the sales price and commission. How would you like to have five closings a month with an average commission of between $4,000 and $6,000 each? As Tom says, "It's a living."

Tom's wife is also an agent and she works mainly with buyers. Naturally, she is an open-house specialist. In picking your strategy, we recommend they be supportive of each other. But we will go into detail on this one in the next chapter.

13 How to Build a Farm

Or, Lessons on How to Keep Your Hands Clean in a Messy Business

This chapter and the next are about the nuts and bolts of executing two particular strategies. To do all six that I mentioned in Chapter 12 would make this book longer than I have time to write or you to read. Still, it is important to see the process worked up a couple of times. Before we start, I must mention an important fact not mentioned in the previous chapter. The two-strategy rule goes out the window after you begin generating more leads than you can handle yourself. Once the lead machine gets going and you bring on sales staff to grow your business, you will want to add strategies. You will still not get to do them all by yourself. Other members of your team who can specialize will do them. Your job will still be lead generation and leadership.

One other caveat: I am discussing the basic processes here. If you are going to succeed in real estate you must keep looking, asking, and reading. What you are getting is a structured, tested approach that will get you going and start you on the path of giving clients great service and making a fine living. Once you master the basics and become productive you will add new ideas and concepts to create your unique practice. But don't get ahead of yourself. Stick with the basic approach until you master it.

Now, we're on to farming.

Sales price is the first factor. As I mentioned before, it is important to select a social grouping that you are comfortable working with. If you sold Lexus cars to the rich and loved it, then farming really upscale areas may be your cup of tea. If you enjoy the upper end of average-income people then select a neighborhood those sorts of people live in. This isn't the rocket-science part. But real estate is not rocket science in any of its parts.

Don't fight for market share

Once you have a target neighborhood selected, the work begins. Let's suppose you are thinking of farming Shavano Park, a solid quarter-million-dollar area. The first task is to pull all the sales in the area for the last two years. What I look for is market dominance. If my report shows that one agent has sold 30% of the homes, I move on to the next neighborhood. The reason for this is simple. In the best of situations, an agent will only get about half the sales in a neighborhood, and it does not matter what you do. A certain number of owners have a relative in real estate or a relationship with a good agent, or have to use the relocation company their employer dictates. This is life, and 50% is the gold standard. If some agent has gotten such a strong position in the area that she can get over halfway to the target 50%, then I would be fighting an uphill battle for agent market share. I would have to spend a lot of money before I get much of a payoff, if I ever did.

The point is few neighborhoods are systematically and professionally marketed, so I look for one with no competition. By the way, I said agent market share. It does not matter if one company has a bunch of sales. Real estate is a personal business and you don't compete against another office, only against other agents. Less than 3% of buyers mention "company" as a factor in selecting an agent. When we were choosing real-estate companies to work for, we looked for a good commission split, great training, and a supportive and positive office environment. We could not have cared less about what the name or market share was.

Turnover is king

The next issue is to compute the average annual turnover rate for the neighborhood. To do this you have to count the total number of houses in the neighborhood. This is time consuming, but there is no way around it. You will need this number for budgeting anyway, so suck it up and count. Divide the number of annual sales by the number of houses and get the percentage. It will be some number between 2% and 12 %, often around 7% to 9%. I want to know if the neighborhood is trending in some direction or stable, so I want to look at three years' worth of percentages. For example, a new area will not hit a maximum rate of turnover until three to five years after construction ends. If a new area is four years old, I expect to see an increase in turnover rate from the second to the third years and again from the third to the fourth years. If this picture does not emerge, I want to investigate further.

The other and more important reason is to find out if the area is suitable for farming in the first place. When I first got into real estate in San Antonio, before Rich joined me in the business, my broker, a nice guy, wanted me to farm Hollywood Park, an upscale, very stable neighborhood. I beat my head against the wall in there and decided I just did not know how to farm. I honestly don't think this broker knew about computing sales percentages or evaluating competition. Later, I computed the turnover rate and it was just over 2%. I found that two agents each had 25% of the market and were battling it out for dominance. This is not enough turnover and too much competition. A good basic number is 7% turnover. With seven homes of every 100 being marketed to going up for sale and becoming a possible listing, I know I have a market for my services. Less than 7% is possible to work, but why bother? The better the turnover, the bigger your marketing reward. I look for significant turnover rates. Remember, marketing costs are figured per household in the farm area, not per sale. Why not work in an area with 7% or even 10% turnover?

One question everyone seems to ask at this point is how big should their farm be. This is a great question but we can't answer it yet. We need a little more specific data—the budget.

The moment of truth

Up to this point in the evaluation we have not spent a nickel. It has all been data collection on the computer. Now the data net gets a bit wider. I have to calculate the cost of the marketing effort on a monthly and annual basis. Here is the moment of truth: if I can't afford to execute the marketing plan for a year, I may as well not even start. Farms usually don't start paying off for a few months. They are not Now business.

Budgeting is easy. As stated earlier, I know that I will have an introductory effort of eight mailings once a week for eight weeks, and then I will send a marketing piece once a month forever. Once a year, I will send an item to go on the refrigerator. This last item could be as simple as our business card with a magnet attached on the back, to the Spurs basketball schedule, or a calendar. I don't think it matters much. The point here is that each item has a cost to create or purchase and a delivery cost. Obviously, the first two months will cost more than an average month, but once I add up the costs I can look at my marketing budget and see if this is a doable project.

Back in Section II, I gave you a straw-man budget to look at. You may want to glance back at it. The point here is that this strategy, geographical farming, requires a fair investment out of pocket to get it off the ground. Of course, it also has some big benefits and payoffs.

Everyone is doing it

Every mega-agent, those with sales numbers in hundreds of units sold per year, has a huge geographical farm. I have read about a few megas who don't have farms, but I have never met one. When you look back at the budget in Section II, glance at Jeff's story again. Once an agent gets mind share in an area, and keeps up the marketing to retain it, she continues getting business. It is all about *getting and keeping*. The big guys would not all do it if it were a losing proposition.

I remember a seminar we went to in 2002. One of the mega-agents from Dallas, a petite 50-something who regularly broke the $60-million annual sales level, was complaining about her sore arms. She and her grown son had delivered Halloween pumpkins to one of her key farm areas the weekend before. Here is a person with GCI numbers in seven digits and she still delivers pumpkins off a rented flatbed truck. This is commitment; this is *keeping*.

One of the factors that make farms attractive is they support other strategies, especially open houses. Once you have a listing in your farm area you are set for high-impact, show-time open houses. I am not going into how to do an open house properly here. But the normal reason to do one is to get in front of buyers. I have never actually sold the house I had open the day of an open house. It happens, but very rarely. However, when the target house is in my farm area I have other objectives besides that day's buyer prospects.

The normal signage for an open house is designed to direct buyers to the property. I make sure all the turns have signs and put balloons on at least the signs on main roads. But in my farm area, I'm going to have neighborhood-specific signs, such as "Another home being sold by The O'Bryant Team." This might be painted on a four- by four-foot piece of plywood in the yard of the open house. I will advertise the munchies inside and do whatever I can for visibility. I want this neighborhood to see the splash and know that I go all out to sell houses.

This open house is a means to reinforce to my market area who I am, and get further into their awareness. It's that mindshare concept again. A lot of people who don't care about my open house will still see the signage, balloons, etc., and three to six months later remember me when they get the relocation notice. Remember, they are also seeing my name on the monthly market update that they get in the mail.

HOAs for mind share

Once you know you are going to farm an area, you want to look for leverage. Leverage is getting more done with less effort. In the case of a geographical farm you may want to look into schools and HOAs. Now I know I have said some unkind things about homeowners associations and I meant every word. But (there is always a but), use them when you can. If the HOA has a newsletter, I want to be prominently featured in it. If they don't have a newsletter, I may want to set up a website to coordinate one and publish it for them. If I publish it, my name is on the front page and the back page. Here is a marketing tip: these newsletters are the sorts of things a lot of people leave lying around in the kitchen or bathroom and if my name is on both sides of it they will see it continuously.

The goal is to be a good neighbor to the HOA even if I don't live in the area. I want to be the area expert, and one way to get to that position is by getting in with the area brain trust, the HOA.

By doing the research I have already done on turnover rates and trends, I have become something of an area expert already. I will want to continue this. At least part of my marketing will include a market update on the neighborhood. Some agents send out recipe cards and cute sayings. These are okay if you like that sort of thing, but I don't do a lot of cooking and don't particularly want people to think of me as the cookie lady. I want to sell houses. Let's get them to think of me as their agent. Knowing some fun facts about an area can be great conversation openers.

In the next chapter I will talk about the biggest moneymaker for our business, but first here are a couple of events that gave us some great fun facts and helped to meet our clients' needs.

Sex and Tax Valuations

In the first farm area that Rich and I did together, he got interested in the county's appraisal district valuations. In this neighborhood, all the houses had been built by the same builder and completed within a three-year period. To his way of thinking, they were about equal in value per square foot if you compared equal-sized homes to each other. Rich could not see why a 1,700-square-foot house on one block should be taxed at $10 per square foot more than the same house a block away. Rich was confused and called an appraiser we knew. The appraiser told us the appraisal district was just out to lunch as usual. Still, Rich couldn't leave it alone.

He researched the appraised valuations on the longest street in the subdivision and started calling the top 10% of appraised values (read highest-taxed homeowners) and the bottom 10% of home owners, those paying the least tax. He took into consideration the allowed deductions for owners over 65 and disabled. The highest-taxed homes were almost all owned by single women. They were not home during the day and Rich could hear kids in the background when he did finally get them on the phone. The lowest-taxed homes tended to be owned by couples at or near retirement with someone home during the day. The picture emerged of single females, heads of household, who were busy. They got the property valuation from the county and saw it as just another bill, like the water or electricity. The older couples saw the tax valuation as an issue to be contested. They went down "to set those appraisal-district people straight," as more than one person said.

We thought this was interesting. Over the next six months we had opportunities to throw this into a lot of conversations with clients and use it in neighborhood marketing pieces. It had the benefit of praising the active citizenship of one group and giving a money-saving tip to the other group.

A Client's Need is a Marketer's Gold

We walked around the first subdivision we farmed. We walked around a lot. If you have more time than money, and we did, we delivered the first marketing pieces ourselves. This had a positive effect. The homeowners started recognizing us and we started getting listings by the second month.

One day Rich was knocking on doors, delivering our new personal brochure; these are better for an agent's ego than his business usually. At one rather average-looking house an old man came to the door and asked Rich in. This happened a lot. We knew a lot of the homeowners in this subdivision were seniors, so Rich was always glad to get to talk to one. He liked to find out what they were thinking, did they like our marketing, etc. This old guy had another issue.

He walked Rich all the way through the house and out the

back door. The deck was a shambles. The cover was rotten and about to fall down and the floor of it was only a little better. The situation looked like the archetypical old person's life. The homeowner, Mr. Cox, was living alone. His wife had passed away two years before, and he was weak and knew it. In fact, he was afraid. He said the deck was a mess and he wanted it torn down before it fell on somebody.

Rich agreed that tearing it down would be the safest thing to do and would make the house more valuable to boot. That was the agent answer; it was not the issue for Mr. Cox.

He said, "If I got a name from the Yellow Pages, I don't know which criminal I'd be inviting into my house." He had read of handymen casing houses for burglars and was concerned.

"What can you do about this, Rich?" Rich did what every astute agent does when asked a question that he doesn't have a clue how to answer; he took Mr. Cox's number and said he would get back to him soon.

Rich told me the story that evening over a glass of wine and we pondered it. The first thing we did was find a good handyman to do the job for Mr. Cox. Rich had already made a couple of calls. But we knew there was a bigger issue here. Keep in mind marketing is a one-way street, us to them. The public, however, is only interested in something that benefits them. Mr. Cox was looking for some help and we figured that if he needed a list of service providers then others did too. How many of those busy single moms needed carpets cleaned, and seniors needed help with yard work, or a painter? A client's need is a marketer's gold, and never forget it. Here was a need looking us in the face.

We put together a vendor list of people we knew were trustworthy, with our name, number, and a disclaimer plastered all over it and sent it out. A lot of people gave this list what we call marketing center stage; they put it on the refrigerator. Needless to say, this got us a lot of loyalty from our vendors as well as increasing mind share with our farm.

14 Circle of Influence as a Major Profit Center

Or, People-Farming for Fun and Profit

Control is a key issue while building a business, and COI offers a great opportunity for this. For example, as we walked around and met people in our geographical farm, a few losers identified themselves. You know, the sour guys who always had a smart or rude comment to make. We dropped them off the mailing list. Life is too short to keep pains in the backside around. In developing a COI, these sorts just never get on in the first place.

The other major issue is consistency.

Before describing the marketing plan, I want to discuss why we developed a people farm. We had several reasons, and in retrospect I see that they were tied to our personalities as much as to anything else. If you are going to do a thing, we figure it should be done well. In fact, it should be done as well as we can do it. That being the case, we did not see any reason for past clients to not refer us business. The only problem was they needed to be reminded from time to time.

Our basic feeling about people is that they don't expect to work with the best agent in the world. They want competent and fair treatment from a knowledgeable, hard-working professional. Once that is established, we would be home free with all the reasonable clients. We never intended to work with the unreasonable any more than the unwashed.

Good models equal great businesses

Earlier, I mentioned that we got a coach very early in our real estate careers. This was a critical step for us. What Joe Stumpf and his By Referral Only organization gave us at the start was a business model to follow. We selected the mailings we wanted to do and followed Joe's model on how often to mail, when to call clients, and how to develop an overall stay-in-touch program. Most of the highly effective steps we do come from

Joe's coaching. If you see some steps that look poorly thought out, well, we have tweaked the systems to fit us over the years.

We did not go out and try to make rocks round, we found a wheel and used it instead.

Some of the names in our database have received our mailings for a decade now. Here is what we do. We provide two mailings a month to the database. One is a simple postcard in which we tell a little story about how we helped some client reach his goal and at the bottom we ask for a referral. The other piece is a letter about some personal issue or value statement that may not even mention real estate at all. One of our best letters was about our ferret's battle with cancer. One of us calls each person a couple of times a year. And we have two client events annually. In the spring we conduct a wine tasting, and in the fall we have an Oktoberfest at the house. For these events we send out very nice invitations and ask for RSVPs. Of course only 10% of Texans know what RSVP means, so it always gets screwed up, but we keep teaching. Each event counts as two touches, one for the invitation and one for the event. This adds up to 31 touches per year and Joe assured us this was not overkill. He was right.

Expense versus value

If you were following my discussion about developing a marketing plan for the geographical farm, you should be saying that this COI is an expensive proposition. Bingo. We spend a considerable sum on each person in the COI database. But there is a very good upside to this.

In his groundbreaking book, *The Millionaire Real Estate Agent*, Gary Keller's research shows that a mature COI database that is marketed to with a consistent 33 touches annually will generate two transactions for every 12 names in the database. This fabulous book is listed in the appendix as a must-read for the professional agent. He goes into this model in great detail. Exactly what the touches are does not seem to matter. Some of the agents Gary polled held client events, some sent letters, newsletters, birthday cards, recipes, you name it; but they did the touches.

In our last year of working full-time in real estate, we sold 71 homes from a database of only 258 people. This is better than two out of 12, and that year we did 93% referrals.

The one thing I will say about the touches is that they must be systematic. I want my mailing pieces to arrive at the COI's homes on the first Saturday and the third Saturday. This has to be like clockwork. They have to know that we are consistent.

As a business-building strategy, you can see from the percentage of return, two sales for every 12 names, 17%, that this is a gold mine for anyone dedicated to providing good service and willing to be consistent. Imagine what your business would be like if you knew you had 50 or 60 transactions in the bag for the year, every year. This could add sanity to it. But a loyal COI has a lot of other payoffs that we don't think about as much as we should.

When Rich retired from the Army, I developed culture shock. For years we had moved around the world and in every new place we instantly had a circle of friends. It seemed as if we were constantly going to parties and meeting new people. With Rich being an instructor at the Command and General Staff College, we had a chance to meet officers from all over the world. It was a blast. When we hit San Antonio, the party ended. We didn't know anyone, and Rich was not on a big staff and didn't have a "high-vis" job. We were just average guys.

That was then. Now we have a huge circle of friends and most came from our COI; they are our past clients. It is that control issue again. We get to pick which people we want to let into our lives and cultivate as friends after the transaction has closed.

26 Miles and $9K

Every year Rich and I do something to give back to the community. Sometimes it is a Christmas project, like the time we organized a gift drive for a nursing home. We taught summer classes at UTSA for under-privileged kids from the south side who planned to go to college in the fall. Well, a few years ago I got the idea of running a marathon for charity, one of those deals where we raise a bunch of money and donate it to a worthy cause while running a marathon for the *fun* of it.

Rich had run a couple of marathons and he assured me that we would have no problems. It was just a long jog and a lot of fun. Of course, he had not done a great deal of running in the last few years, and it had been 14 years since he had actually run a long distance. A lot of people do them, though, so they must be doable.

The cause we chose was one close to my heart, leukemia research. We felt that this was both a worthy cause and one that a lot of people could identify with. The fund-raising target for both of us together was $9,000. Rich felt a lot more capable of running the distance than raising the money. I was worried, but I knew the only way to success is to start. Since Rich is a good cook and I'm a marketer, we did two spaghetti lunches in the office and invited title companies, inspectors, and whoever else we could think of. Rich cooked up the pasta and four different sauces, gallons of them. We charged $5 a plate and sold almost 500 plates, which got us almost halfway to the goal. One of our past clients got his company to donate the pasta and tomato sauce. The rest of the funds came from our mailing campaign.

Between the long runs six days a week and selling real estate, we sent out letters to the COI asking for help and asking if anyone had had any involvement with this terrible form of cancer. We did not know what we were getting into.

The letters and checks poured in. We reached our goal with time to spare, but it was the letters that got us. So many of these people we knew, whom we had worked with, had stories that literally made us cry. We knew we had a good cause to work for, but we had not realized how widespread this terrible disease is. The education alone made doing this event worthwhile. But that was only the beginning.

When we told our assistant that we were doing a larger-than-average project and laid it out for her, she balked. Within three weeks she was offered a job at her old brokerage office back and left us. She felt that with all of these distractions, our business would hit the wall before we ever started the race, which was five months down the road in October. On one level she was right. The next five months were hard. Between the running, thank-you notes to donors, and selling real estate, we did not have a lot of breaks.

It was our best year in the business.

Because we did not have time to spare, we planned more carefully. It was that simple. Since that time we have had a hard time saying we are too busy for anything, or accepting that excuse from anyone else.

As luck would have it, Rich damaged his knee after a training run. He was getting into the car and twisted his knee funny after an easy eight-mile run at Camp Bullis. He had torn the cartilage in it the first time in 1968 at Ft. Benning and had bunged it several times since. So during the marathon, he and another non-running husband rode up and down the course on motor scooters, providing moral support.

The big issue is the way that our Circle of Influence jumped in and helped. We thought they just wanted us as agents—we found out that they accepted and valued us as people.

ಐ

Wedding Day

It was June, love was in the air, and the wedding season was in full swing. A dear friend and client, Maria, called: "Hey, the wedding is June tenth—be there!"

Of course, we said we would go. A few days later, an invitation arrived in the mail: "Dick and Shelly are getting married on June 10!"

We promptly sent back the positive RSVP. It wasn't until we were writing dates in the planner that we realized that both weddings were on the same day.

Well, that wasn't too bad. One was at 4:00 and the other was at 6:00. We were okay, since most weddings only last 30 to 45 minutes, we'd have plenty of travel time in between. And that was a good thing. The first one was in Castroville, a good 40 minutes out of town, while the second was at Trinity University in downtown San Antonio.

We arrived at the church for the first wedding at 3:45. It was a beautiful day. The church was a classic little Catholic church in the old German community. The architecture and the stained-glass windows with Gothic German script seemed to have been designed to take us back to the old country, to the Europe of another century.

The bride and groom were both Gonzaleses, the priest Irish. It was a lovely multi-cultural event and the place was packed. At 4:00 the groom and priest started getting antsy; normally the bride and bridesmaids would be lining up at the back of the church by now. By 4:15, they decided to sit down, since the bride was nowhere in sight.

At 4:25, amid some dust and to a lot of relief, the limo arrived. The bride and her five bridesmaids tumbled out, somewhat disheveled, and ran straight to their places. The organist caught the cue and struck up the Mendelssohn March; the bride was at last coming down the aisle. Later, the story of the tardy hair stylist and limo were widely circulated, but given little credibility. Maria was born late and stayed that way.

The atmosphere relaxed noticeably, except for us. If the wedding went on longer than 30 minutes, we'd be late for the next wedding! The priest began with a comment on their long engagement: "Maria has been waiting two years for this day. Hector has been waiting for this day for two years and twenty-five minutes!"

We couldn't stand it; the whole audience broke into laughter, as did the groom. The priest thought it unseemly to laugh at his own joke and proceeded. The thousand-year-old mystery of the mass unfolded with strong Irish intonations.

Sure enough, the ceremony, being Catholic, ran long—mysteries take time. We hurried out as soon as the receiving line was formed with promises to the bride and groom that we would see them at the reception.

We got to the second wedding by 6:02. The bride was just approaching the altar. We'd made it just in time, and the setting couldn't have been more different. The female minister stood to the right of the altar. Dick and Shelly, with single attendants, were standing oblique to the crowd so that the audience could participate in the event as if it were a play. The church continued this dramatic theme with eclectic modern lighting and music that was classical rather than traditional. It was clear we had moved from the twelfth century to the twenty-first.

As soon as the ceremony ended, we headed downtown for the first reception. It was a huge temptation to just blow it off, but we had committed to go, and so we went. No one would believe that we did not know what RSVP meant. They served a full meal with fish and meat, vegetables, salad, the whole works. It was beautiful. There was a big mariachi group and then a 20-piece orchestra. It must have cost a mint to throw this party. It was a Hispanic grand time in the best Texas tradition.

As we looked around the room, we became especially glad we had come. It was heartbreaking to see at least eight empty tables of eight places each. Sadly, it is also typical for people to promise to attend, then not show up. How many hundreds of dollars had been spent on people who hadn't come?

Much too soon, we had to leave for the second reception, not wanting to arrive too late and contribute to another empty table. Full and happy, we left for the second party. It was packed. The music was rock and roll, the beer was European, and the food had a decided nouveau-cuisine style. It was also in the best Texas tradition. Perhaps because they had booked a much smaller reception hall, the place had barely an empty seat.

America is continuing to blend and diversify at the same time. In one day, we saw tradition and we saw the 21st century expressed, and both worked. Just like our country, it works.

An old Englishman commented in 1887, " The French have too little individual liberty, while the Americans have too much!" I don't know if we have too much, but we do have a lot.

ಬ

V Work Toward Mailbox Money

Or, Leave During the Applause

> *What shelter to grow ripe is ours?*
> *What leisure to grow wise?*
> —Matthew Arnold

"Real estate is what I do, not who I am," is one of Joe Stumpf's favorite sayings, and we value it. This is not to say real estate is not important or that we do not appreciate it greatly. Rather, it is just part of our lives and does not comprise the whole. This is important to keep in mind and helpful when it comes to putting events into perspective. In the next couple of chapters we will consider growing your business into a team and working yourself out of a job. At the end, I have some thoughts about escaping the working world that may be worth consideration.

My point here is that my life has goals, it has an aim that includes freedom to explore myself, time to learn about life, and room to grow into the person I must become. This lofty goal requires a lot of support, and that is where my business fits into my life. When we fully exploit it, we will have the support structure in place so that our lives can continue to expand. This is what I mean when I say business is the support of life, not the thing we live for.

Much of what I have to say is covered at length in Michael E. Gerber's book, *The E-Myth Revisited* (see the appendix). This is an easy-to-read, great book and a new edition has recently been published.

15 Build It Right and It Will Last

Many of us spend a lot of life waiting to figure out the big picture. We make excuses for our inactivity by pretending that we will get mountains scaled, careers accomplished, and Armageddon fought as soon as we figure out all the details. At times it almost seems like a conspiracy that everyone else knows what they are doing and here I sit still trying to figure it out. Well there is a secret you need to know. They don't know any more than you do. Maybe less.

There is a famous passage in Ulysses S. Grant's memoirs. The governor had given a private citizen and dry-goods salesman, Grant, the rank of colonel so that he could run his state's recruiting effort. (The Army later confirmed this commission; Grant had graduated from West Point.) Soon he found himself in command of a large brigade charged with attacking a strong rebel force some miles away. Grant comments how frightened he was at the prospect of leading men into battle, a new thing for him. During the Mexican War in 1845, he had only reached the rank of captain and had been a quartermaster.

He had accurate reports that the enemy position was just over the next hill. With his heart in his throat, he spurred his horse on. When he crested the rise and peered into the valley below, he saw the wreckage of a large, recently and hastily evacuated camp. The enemy was afraid too. This was an epiphany for Col. Grant. In later years, his fear would still come, but now it was always manageable.

Know what a risk is

By sticking to the plan, we built a business that was predictable. Every year we know how many leads the database will generate. As we add strategies and change our business plan, we deepen its predictability. As Kiyosaki says in his book, *Rich Dad, Poor Dad*, "The investment is not risky. It's the lack of simple financial intelligence." Planning and executing a strategy as we have described here is not risky. Not having a plan is disaster.

One of the planning steps we did early on was lay out an organizational chart, and I still have one for my current business. At first the same names were in all the boxes and it looked a bit dumb, but it wasn't. Humans have to see a thing to believe in it. Writing up what the organization looks like when it is built, three or five years down the road, is critical. Every day I go to work I see my business as it will be three years from now and work every day to build that business. Here is a distinction. I am building that future business, not just working in my business.

Now, let's get back to the ground.

You have seen the productive possibilities of a geographical farm and a COI. If we sold 71 houses from a database of 258, what are the possibilities for a database of 500 or 5,000? If 500 homes can generate 17 sales per year, what if I can develop some economies of scale, as Jeff did, and farm 25,000 homes? You can do these things. You can because others have *already* done them. The reason they could is that they have a business mindset and understand two important points.

Don't wait for facts

They discovered that if you can budget it, you can do it. An entrepreneur never has all the facts before he begins; often he just begins and trusts that everyone else has the same issues he does. He just knows he will succeed because he will keep trying. The second thing successful agents know is that their clients are not in love with *them*. The clients want the service. It is the high standards of customer service that attract and keep clients for life. If an agent can systemize her business in such a manner that others can provide the service, then the business can grow exponentially.

Remember the organizational chart with your name in all the blocks? Well, some agents have grown their business to the point that they replaced themselves right out of it. For instance, there are the McKissacks. This focused couple started out as just Linda doing a mediocre job as an agent. She got a little better, and her husband went bankrupt in his business and joined her so that they could pay off nearly six digits of debt. Today, they spend a lot of time opening real estate offices around the country and building other businesses such as title companies, mortgage companies, and property management firms. Jim only spends 2 hours a week in their personal real-estate business and Linda less than that. Still, it sells $45 million worth of homes a year and is continuing to grow. Both have actually replaced themselves in their own business.

How is that for a goal?

At a convention recently, Gary Keller, founder of Keller Williams Realty, said that to build a really big business the CEO has to have enough faith in his systems and standards "to get out of the way and let it grow as big as it needs to be."

After you build the business, what do you do then? This is a great question, and I want to give two answers, but I will start by relating an incident.

Where's my dentist?

A few weeks ago a friend of ours stopped by and we were passing the time, catching up. He mentioned that he had gone to his dentist the previous day. That did not sound as exciting as some other activities, so I waited for the punch line and started thinking of new topics. Getting teeth whitened is not worth the time to discuss. He said he went into the office and everything happened just like it always had. The same cute assistant took the x-rays and got him ready for the checkup and then a strange guy came into the treatment room. Instead of a tall, gray-headed guy, here was a short fellow who was probably from Bombay.

He asked, "What happened to my dentist?" and was told the other dentist had retired and he, Dr. Singh, was the dentist now, and "please open your mouth wide." The new guy was a good dentist and our friend made a follow-up appointment to get some drilling done.

Of course, what had happened was the new guy had bought the old dentist's practice. The new doctor will pay the old one a percentage of profit for a set period of time. This rewards the first dentist for building a business and allows the new guy to jump on a moving train and get going quickly. This trend is out there and it is moving into real estate. Those agents who have built strong, loyal databases and have good documented systems in place will be able to sell their practices just as our friend's dentist did.

If you want something a bit more solid, then stay with me as we go to the best leveraging you can do with your money and expertise.

16 Rentals are a Lot of Work

Or, Letting Your Knowledge and Money Multiply Your Wealth

This chapter is just a suggestion. What I want you to consider is your vision of the business you are building. In the concluding section of this book, we will go into detail on envisioning your business, but for now let's focus on the future, on our exit strategy. It doesn't matter if you are in real estate or golf-course management, the topic is the same. Someday I will either not want to work as much or not be able to work as much. The only choice any of us have is whether we will control what happens or just let it happen. Calendars don't lie, and time doesn't stop.

Every step we have discussed so far has a single goal, to give you tools to visualize different components of your business. What will it look like when it is finished? If you cannot envision your lead-generation system you cannot plan to implement it. Not a complicated concept. Every action begins as a thought and every business has three executable components and a final outcome. It stands to reason that any business owner must have a very clear picture of these three doable parts: marketing (lead generation), operations (what I do that people want), and finance (am I getting rich or going broke?). The final outcome, or goal if you think that way, of the endeavor must also be envisioned and planned.

The future is not optional

If we carry this concept forward, I have to look at my entire business and the time frame I have to execute it. If I'm 25 years old, I can plan on more years to execute a plan than if I'm 55. What will you do when you want to, or have to, stop practicing your profession? Even if you don't accept anything else I discuss in this chapter, I want you to take to heart one observation: You will never be able to see your business accurately, or thoroughly understand your goals for it, until you can see how it will provide an exit plan for you and your family. Pretending you will never age only plays in Hollywood. However, if you don't care for my suggestion, that's okay; all you have to do is come up with a better one. Here are our thoughts on the subject and part of our vision for post-career O'Bryant Team.

When I mention owning rental property the usual response is that rent houses are a lot of work. The inflection people use has an overtone of "don't play in the street; it's dangerous." It is as though they believed they were imparting some actual information. Of course, on one level they are right. However, I have another perspective and it is perspective that makes all the difference.

In my life I have been a single mom, paid my own college tuition, bought my own house, and built something of a career. Marrying Rich made life more fun, but I was *making it* when we met. One thing stands out: I have never found very much money lying around. To this day our income depends on work that we have done or are currently doing. Of course, owning investment properties involves work. Selling real estate isn't bon-bons in the hot tub either. *Everything is work.*

Another fact of life is that everything in my life is an outcome of options. Every decision is little more than a choice of one option over another and once that has happened, the options not selected are gone. Bear with me here. If I decide to cross the street and do it, I have lost the option of staying put. I know this isn't profound yet, but I'm only warming up. If the client buys the house on Naked Indian Road then he can't live in the one on Timberline.

At some point all of us will want to not work, and we will want economic stability. In the example of the homebuyer, we know that his choice is not just an open-ended decision. The guy has to have done a few things before his choice will mean anything. Not complicated stuff, but qualifying for a loan is common, as are having an income or being of legal age. This applies to choosing to not work and still have food with your meals. Let's look at this.

Value isn't advertised

On the way to discussing rental property, I want to make a couple of unoriginal observations. I'm not saying that you don't already know this; actually, I'm positive you do. But I want you to understand where I'm coming from, as my youngest son would say. The options for retirement planning such as IRAs, Roths, and the like fall into the general category of Better Than Nothing. Or as Rich says (he is so always to the point), they are like the stuff advertised to clean the lime build-up in coffee pots. The stuff works, but it cost $3.49 before tax, and 25 cents worth of vinegar does the job better. Ever wonder why the big stock brokerages advertise their IRA products during the Super Bowl? They do it because they need to! These are the $3.49 products that are not as good as the 25-cent ones. I'm cheap, but I also know that a problem exists that is not easily overcome.

In the case of using vinegar to clean a coffee pot, the problem is that no one is advertising this to the public *and no one ever will*. There is no money in it for the advertiser—vinegar is a low-margin product and manufacturers can't invest in it. For the same reason you will not see primetime advertisements recommending that agents invest in real estate. But look at your assets, knowledge, and opportunities.

Some years ago Rich got on a stock-buying kick. To this day, we have $6,200 in a money-market account waiting for him to jump in. Being the person he is, Rich started reading books by some of the big names in the industry. He wanted to be an expert. Very soon he came to Peter Lynch and his superb book, *Beating the Street*. Here was a guy even I could identify with. When he heard about a small motel chain in Texas named La Quinta that was beating up on the local Holiday Inns, Lynch spent a few nights in a couple of them. Then he checked out the earnings and cash position of the company and bought a bunch of stock. The price doubled nine times in the next decade. Lynch said, "Buy what you know." Naturally, this guy knew about a lot of stocks and when Rich and I discussed what to buy at our evening wine conference, we hit an immediate problem. We did not know any stocks. Sure, we liked some companies but just by looking I can't tell if Costco's per-store operation is any better than Sam's Club's. Of course, this is not what Lynch was talking about. However, we do know a lot about valuing investments, just not about stocks.

We bought another rent house.

One other point I want you to think about when planning your exit strategy from the working world is that investing should not be risky. To us the stock markets seem risky. We don't have any control over what happens there. All the information about companies, their stocks, investment instruments, and available cash reserves are managed by individuals in corporations or hired by the corporations. These folks have vested interests in how the numbers look. That reminds me of coffee pot cleaner; I still want to use vinegar.

Because I am a real-estate professional, I can value a house, get rental comparables, and get a quality inspection. I even know a bunch of craftsmen to call if I need estimates on repairs. In fact I can't think of any critical elements of information that I can't get before I buy an investment property. I can even know how long it will take to rent it. The average days on market are valid numbers based on the input of many different agents. About the only thing I can't know ahead of time is the name of the tenant. And this investment will be done on my timetable.

When you're ready, it happens

We don't spend a lot of time looking for investment properties. When a good situation presents itself, if we are ready to take advantage of it, we act. Let's face it, agents look at houses every day. If you think you do not see great deals every week let me suggest something to you. Save $9,000 and have it in a savings account and go to a lender and get pre-approved for an investment loan. The deals will come out of the woodwork. They are there now, but you are not ready to see them, so they are invisible—to you!

Personally, I like to put significant down payments on investment properties, but this exercise will get you going. Remember what I said about your listing presentation 10 chapters ago. If you don't have confidence in the presentation, your subconscious will not let you give it. Your brain will find a way to avoid listing presentations so that you will not embarrass yourself. On the other hand, if you have a great presentation, your subconscious brain will help get you in front of clients to give it. In the same way, when you are ready for a great deal, you will find one.

Just money or time

The showstopper in real-estate investing is fear of the known. We have all seen the problems that can happen in real estate and we want to avoid them. Good idea. I find that we generally don't have problems with investment properties and the serious investors I work with don't either. When I go into a deal I know a few unforeseen things will happen. So what? Everything that we generally call a problem is no more than a situation requiring a little more time or a few more bucks. The end of the world doesn't happen. This is not to say you or I can skip doing our homework before a purchase (see the next story.)

The next thing you are going to ask about is how I set up a real-estate investment portfolio that will be wildly profitable. I'm not going to do that because it would not be beneficial. Gary Keller has published *The Millionaire Real Estate Investor*, a 407-page book that discusses this process from all the important perspectives. In it, he and the co-authors provide pricing charts, inspection costing lists, and detailed explanations of the different aspects of investing. It is not a book that must be read cover to cover, but I did. The table of contents is clear, and you can easily find chapters on whatever issues you have.

This is important. I have to have an information resource to avoid deadly doubt and expensive procrastination. Two of my absolute beliefs are: first, that at the end of my days the things I will feel worst about are those that I wished I had done and not the mistakes that I learned from and never repeated. Second, the only things that will matter are those I did; should-have-dones will offer no solace.

Not every investment story is a 100% success. In this little story we see that a certain amount of care is required, even with a killer system.

Always Check the Back Door

Recently, Rich and I had breakfast with an investor friend, Jerry, from the Houston area. He has a very successful real-estate practice and owns several related businesses. As a profitable sideline, he and a partner buy investment properties. One of his favorite strategies is to buy stuff cheap at auction on the courthouse steps.

His system is slick. First, he went to the auction and made notes. Who were the regular players, who could pick value, and who were the determined buyers? The first fact that jumped out was that it was a clique. The same old boys showed up every auction and the same people were players every month. Then Jerry got his money together. He wanted to play.

Not being a person to take money from savings, he refinanced a few of his rent houses and "harvested some equity," as he put it. To purchase at the auction, cash is required so he got his cash together. The next step was to line up two banks. Jerry had accounts with several banks already. For his strategy he needed to use one for holding the cash and issuing money orders. The second was needed to finance the houses he bought and wanted to keep.

Actually buying the houses was simple.

Jerry or his partner got the list of county foreclosures and checked out the ones they were interested in. This was not a subjective do-I-like-it call. They worked out a written set of criteria and applied it to every house. With the foreclosure list and a property tax printout in hand, they looked at the houses.

On auction day, Jerry draws $200,000 in cashier's checks of varying amounts from the first bank and goes to the bidding. If a targeted house actually goes up for sale, he buys it as long as its price is not over the maximum price he and his partner have set for the house. They will not buy a house that is not 20% under market value.

The system works well 80% of the time and okay the rest of the time, and that is good enough. But one month they got in a hurry. One particular house was priced beautifully and met all the criteria. It was brick with three bedrooms, two baths, and a garage. It would probably rent easily and appreciate in value with the market.

Jerry thought it odd that no one bid against him on this one. He got it for his first offer and paid the clerk cash as required. All sales are final.

When Jerry had a minute a couple of days later, he went by the house to work up a punch list for his remodeling contractor. Every house needs some work and he expected it. This house was in good shape, except the back wall was missing.

Somehow the entire back wall of the place had been ripped off and hauled away. He had never known of a house missing an entire exterior wall.

I'm not sure which Jerry minded more, the cost of fixing up the place, or the stories the other bidders were telling about him. But he was not happy. Replacing the wall cost all of the profit and a ton of time, but he checks things more closely now and doesn't get in a hurry.

଼

17 Planning for Success From the Start

Or, You're Going to Spend the Time Anyway, So Why Not Do It Profitably?

So far, our discussion has covered buyers, sellers, lead generation, and customer service. I have told 18 stories and asked you to look at your business as it will be when you have developed it as far as you plan to go. Then we spent some time considering my thoughts on how to survive after real estate, in fact after all active business. Looks like we have a few loose strings to tie up and a summary to end with. From a practical perspective, no one can pull together a concept as complicated as a real-estate practice in one concluding chapter of a short book. But I can try.

Every business has the three basic components: marketing, operations, and finance.

Marketing, or whatever you select for lead generation, must be focused. Because there are only six general ways to make money in this business you will have to pick one or two. I suggest you pick two. Rich and I finally settled on open houses and Circle of Influence (COI). After a few years we gradually dropped open houses and concentrated on COI and selling our listings. It was not that doing open houses did not work. But, if you really learn *any* strategy up to the mastery level, it will take you to a nice six-digit GCI. On the human front, it is hard to work a bunch of Sunday afternoons when you don't have to.

The devil in marketing is, as it is in everything, doubt, which fosters indecision. Jane Doeson, the woman I described in the introduction, did not fail because she was dumb. If anything, she was too bright. Every class she attended had a new idea and she had to try it. She did so much new stuff she never mastered the old stuff. Then she ran out of the green stuff and had to get a j-o-b.

In the area of marketing, we wrote out an organizational chart of our entire marketing plan. We listed who would do every job and every task in this area. Rich then worked up a spreadsheet of the costs on a monthly and annual basis. I plugged this into QuickBooks and we about had our financial planning done.

Operations are more complicated than you would think. The complications come in because this is a critical part of marketing as well as serving clients. As with marketing, we did an organizational chart of all the functions to be done in the client-care area. To this we added the best checklists we could get our hands on. I found out early on that life was more fun if I got checklists from experts. An expert was anyone doing three or four times as much business as we were, and I modified checklists to suit our situation. To do one from scratch meant we left something out. Happened every time. If you don't know a good agent in your market area, then get what you need out of a Tom Hopkins book or Keller's *The Millionaire Real Estate Agent*. But whatever you do, don't spend a week trying to write your own.

After the checklists we added the scripts. Joe Stumpf, our referral coach, has hundreds of them and we selected the ones we needed and stuck them into the organizational chart where they needed to go. Rich and I went over them so often that clients heard the same approach from both of us. They knew we had systems and felt comfortable that we were professionals.

Here is the complicated part I mentioned earlier. If a client is pleased with the service she is getting, about half the time she will refer another person to us if properly asked. A 50% referral rate during the transaction is the gold standard of referrals, but even at just halfway to the goal we were getting a huge benefit.

Leads for free

Think about the cost to generate enough leads to get a closing. Suppose half of those closings gave you your next deal. Your marketing cost per closing would drop like a rock, and profitability would act like a cat on a hot stove—it would jump.

At this point, I have an organizational chart of our

marketing plan and operation with a list of everything we will do in each area and the scripts to support the activities. Now we are ready to do two things. Most importantly, we are ready to make money. Our business mindset has moved us to the point that we can acquire client mind share. We have procedures to learn and scripts to practice. After we reach mastery, we will have the opportunity to grow. This is the second issue. Not everyone wants to make the emotional investment of Mary Harker or Jimmy and Linda McKissack and build a big team. But let's stop for a second and consider just what these organizational tools do for us.

Michael Gerber advises us to replace ourselves in our organization. If you look at each job that needs to be done, you will see that you don't like doing some of them. At about the same time it will occur to you how you can leverage yourself out of doing the ones you least like to do. Some can be outsourced to a printing company or cleaning team, or you can hire someone on a per-job or part-time basis. When you start doing that, and if you use the freed-up time to get even more focused on lead generation, you will grow. The normal result is a team. The McKissacks gradually filled all the blocks in their organizational chart and now just provide the vision and some training. The machine keeps producing and they don't have to be around every day for it to continue doing so.

Concluding Thoughts

We have come full circle and returned to the Business Owner Mindset, our main objective. Before we could build our real-estate practice, we had to envision it at all the levels. We learned to do the nuts and bolts of the business in marketing and operations.

To grow we had to envision what our business would look like at various points in the future. Finally, we had to agree on our exit strategy and start implementing it. Of course, it did not happen smoothly. At the beginning, we did not know what we know now. Who does? But it has been a fulfilling trip so far.

The satisfaction of creating something, the relationships, and most importantly the increased self-awareness has given us back so much more than we gave. Our business has given us a bigger life, as yours can do for you.

Appendix

Reading list, or a place to start

What follows is a short list of books that I think every beginning agent should consider and all of us should revisit from time to time. Some books, like Gary Keller's and Tom Hopkins's, fall into two categories. They are great books to read as general background for our real estate careers. They are also reference books with workable tables of contents and indexes for easy research on specific topics. As I've mentioned several times, don't try to invent something if one of the masters has already done it. If you need a dialog, check out Hopkins; if you need to set up a table of accounts in QuickBooks, check out the sample Profit and Loss Report in Appendix A of Keller's *MREA*. Real estate is probably the second- or third-oldest profession in civilization—trust me, somebody has done everything before.

The comments I have made about each book listed below are not meant as a critical review or a book report. These are just some remarks that may help you decide which one to read first. The books are arranged alphabetically by author, not in order of merit or the order you should consider reading them. At the end of the list are some comments about my coaches.

DNA Leadership Through Goal-Driven Management, by James R. Ball

This book has been around a few years and is still actively selling on Amazon.com. Mr. Ball uses the DNA model to provide a systematic approach to establishing goals for both individuals who want to accomplish a lot in life and for organizations. This is not the book you read to learn how to do anything in real estate, but it is a great resource for getting all of your team on the same page and/or your life on track. Rich and I read this book at least seven years ago and we still discuss it and refer to it.

The Roaring 2000s Investor, by Harry Dent, Jr.

This book, strictly speaking, is not about real estate or the real estate profession. However, Dent is an analytical sort who looks closely at demographic trends, population shifts, immigration, and growth rate projections. I think it is worth your consideration on two counts. First, knowing about the mega-trends that drive growth rates can't hurt you and may give you some insight on your own investments or selecting a financial advisor. The other thing is that it has a ton of facts and information that can make a newbie sound like a long-time student of the market.

The E-Myth Revisited, by Michael E. Gerber

We are born with a lot of good stuff in our heads and we get more from family and friends as we develop. However, we aren't born knowing how to set up a real estate practice on sound business principles. We have to learn this and Gerber is the teacher. In our story in Section II, Jeff replaces himself in his business and gets a life. This is what Gerber discusses: how to build your business.

How to Master the Art of Listing Real Estate, by Tom Hopkins

Hopkins is old-school real estate. This book's copyright is from the 80s, and some of the details are a bit out of date. So what? Hopkins discusses setting up binders to file stuff and folders for presentations. You will probably use your PC for that. But the fact remains, if you set up a listing presentation to be as well-organized and scripted as he demonstrates in this book, you will get listings. It is that simple. You may want to use PowerPoint and not a three-ring binder; those are just details. He also goes into i-dotting and t-crossing detail on setting up geographical farms, open houses, and all the rest. Compare what he says to *MREA* and you will have a very clear picture of our industry.

How to Master the Art of Selling, by Tom Hopkins

I love a presumptuous title, but this one really isn't. Here Hopkins gets into the nuts and bolts of selling. His sections on objection handling, prospecting, and closing techniques are classics.

The Millionaire Real Estate Agent, by Gary Keller

This is a big book and it includes some very sophisticated concepts, but the premise is simple. If you base your business on the correct models, you will be able to grow it as big as it needs to get. If you are only going to read one book on the real estate industry, this is the one. Mr. Keller got together three seminar groups of high-quality agents over a period of two years and developed this best-practice compilation. (Rich and I were in one of these groups and they were intense.) Then he put together a research team to literally travel all over the country interviewing the top performers to validate his research. The bottom line is that this book is not someone's opinion or what some guy believes, it is a well-researched presentation of the best practices in the industry. Could you ask for more?

The Millionaire Real Estate Investor, by Gary Keller

This book proves that Mr. Keller is no more original in his book titles than Hopkins. However, it is an important book on two fronts. The first and most obvious is that as real estate professionals, we are in the best possible place to capitalize on investing in real estate. This book covers the subject from mindset to maintenance. Second, it is my belief that in the coming decade we will see continuing interest in real estate investment by the general public. This means that you will have investor clients to advise. After spending a few evenings with this book you will be able to sound sensible to even the most experienced investor. Being able to sound like Robert Kiyosaki is something for every new agent to consider.

Rich Dad, Poor Dad, by Robert T. Kiyosaki

Every list of books needs an easy read and this one is it. Kiyosaki does not discuss our profession except to say that real estate investors need to use our services. I have included him because of his outlook on risk assessment, investing, and planning. Of course, anyone with three books on the Wall Street Journal's bestseller list at one time is probably okay. I have found clients to be receptive to his arguments. This is the book you read to motivate yourself to read Keller's investing book. Kiyosaki has written a number of other books, many with specialists in other fields, and they are worth your time.

The 22 Immutable Laws of Branding, by Al Ries and Laura Ries,
The 22 Immutable Laws of Marketing, by Al Ries and Jack Trout

These two books may not be the first books you read about business organization. For a beginning agent and businessperson, the basic planning that Gerber and Keller provide is more critical. However, before you get very far down the road of business building, you will want to know how marketing and branding systems work. These two books are very short, and the authors have gone out of their way to be direct and to the point. I have found them to be a good resource to review before taking action. Rules exist in these areas and they are not always based on common sense.

Secrets of Closing the Sale, by Zig Ziglar

To my knowledge, Ziglar has never sold a house, but don't hold that against him. I have had the opportunity to hear him speak a couple of times, once on stage with Tom Hopkins, and he is a master. This book deconstructs the selling process and considers salesmanship from the bottom up. In one section he even discusses the percentages of the population who have the psychological profile to become salespeople. Ziglar has written a ton of books on selling. This one covers most of his main points on the topic. You will not be able to put it down.

Coaches and mentors

Joe Stumpf, founder of By Referral Only and my real estate business coach

In the text, I have mentioned Joe several times and I have provided his contact information below. This charismatic leader gave Rich and me the model for our business, a model we believed in and were excited to execute. Without Joe's help we may not have even stayed in the business, much less been successful at it.

As the name of his organization implies, many of the systems he has researched and developed focus on developing a Circle of Influence for referrals, but that isn't all. Many mortgage lenders and financial planners have joined his coaching program, too. Most of the scripts and dialogs we use for lead conversion, client referral training, and objection handling come from his instructions. Of course, these fit perfectly with his lead generation and business operations models.

Joe is not the only coach available, and you may be more satisfied with someone else's personality. My suggestion is to check a few out. The two points I want to make are first, that your coach should help you execute the strategy you have selected for your business (COI, FSBO, farming, etc.). If your goal is just lead conversion and closing a deal, then Joe Stumpf's approach, with his heavy emphasis on client care and being referable, may not line up with your objectives as well as another would.

Second, I don't think you should get excited about what a great coach costs. If you will close 60 deals instead of 20 and have systems in place that allow you to have a life with your career, the price does not matter. Rich and I do not believe any coach we have had has ever cost us anything, yet our checking account is debited monthly.

To contact By Referral Only, you can go to their website, www.byreferralonly.com, or call them at 1-800-950-7325. Joe has graciously offered a free one-hour business development consultation with one of his highly-talented business consultants for anyone calling and mentioning this book.

Alicia Fruin, President of Profit Consulting Co. and my other business coach

I know I probably don't *need* two coaches, but I have known Alicia for many years and knew that her coaching style would benefit me and my business. We work on a wide range of issues, including personal ones as well as business development. She has coached many businesses and individual professionals across the country. If you need to give your organization a personalized push up the ladder to greater focus and productivity, or to just get yourself organized, give her a call and discuss it. She has also offered a free one-hour consultation. Give her a call at 1-512-989-2230 or at Alicia@profitconsultingco.com.

About the authors

Pam O'Bryant

Pam brings a unique combination of real estate and teaching experience to the creation of this book. In real estate, Pam has had a wide range of experience, from overseeing condo conversions in the Washington, DC, metroplex to building a solid and profitable residential sales business in San Antonio with her husband Rich. Her educational background includes a BS Ed. in Spanish and a master's degree in teaching English as a second language. In real estate, she has her broker's license and has participated in numerous seminars with leaders in the field as well as continuing coaching relationships with several national-level trainers.

While developing her personal real estate practice, Pam played a critical role in developing the continuing education program for the 150-agent office she worked in. Over a three-year period, Pam developed and taught dozens of classes and organized a program based on the concept of the top agents sharing and mentoring newer agents. The expressed goal of the program was to help even newer agents build very profitable businesses. This program is still in place and prospering.

Her "alma mater" real estate office now holds the licenses of 300 full-time agents, is hugely profitable, and continues to offer business-building training classes four days a week. It is the years of hands-on training and mentoring agents to build bigger and better practices that form the basis of this book.

Pam's orientation is productivity. Success is not about being right, but getting the right things done.

About Rich O'Bryant

Rich is another case; prior to marrying Pam, his only contact with the real estate community had been a few home purchases. After retiring from the Army after 22 years, Rich decided to get into real estate with Pam. He figured they made a great team, and he couldn't think of a better way to use his master's degree in

Early Modern European History!

Rich has one thing in common with Pam: he has a strong teaching background. In the military, he taught at the Command and General Staff College for three years and has conducted dozens of classes for agents in various facets of the business, from listing presentations to lead conversion.

Rich's specialty is in personality profile assessments and helping agents not only in determining their personal preferences, but in using that information to build a sustainable business that will be fun into the future. He is very knowledgeable in the DISC and Myers-Briggs assessment tools.

What's next for *Scorpion*?

Scorpion in the Toolbox, our next book, is coming out in the summer of 2006. It will cover prospecting and agent career development.

While this current book focused on organizing your real estate business and deciding on the basic strategies you will use to grow it, the next book will be like a toolbox. We will provide very specific guidance on *how* and *when* to prospect, and we'll tailor our guidance to specific strategies. Every seminar instructor we have ever paid to teach us about sales has preached about prospecting. But none of them has ever told us exactly what to do during the two hours of our day that we can control. We will, and we'll include stories to illustrate every step, because you can't learn if you aren't smiling.

Until then, here are some words to live by: "Nobody ever quit real estate because they had too many quality leads."

By the way, we love stories and would love to read yours (and perhaps use them). If you have had a *Scorpion in the Bathtub* experience, please take a moment to contact us at info@scorpionbooks.com and tell us about it.

CPSIA information can be obtained
at www.ICGtesting.com
Printed in the USA
FSOW02n2241250916
25398FS

9 781598 008913